The
Louisville
Review

Number 91
Spring 2022

THE LOUISVILLE REVIEW

Editor	Sena Jeter Naslund
Associate Editor	Flora K. Schildknecht
Managing Editor	Amy Foos Kapoor
Guest Poetry Editor	Jonathan Weinert
Guest Fiction Editor	Beth Ann Bauman
Cornerstone Editor	Betsy Woods
Technical Director	Ron Schildknecht
Financial Director	John Morgan

TLR publishes two volumes each year: spring and fall. Visit our website for complete guidelines, back issues, subscriptions, and more: www.louisvillereview.org.

Like us on Facebook for up to date information about each issue, news on contributors, etc.: www.facebook.com/TheLouisvilleReview. Follow us on Twitter @TheLouRev.

Questions? Please note our email and mailing addresses:

managingeditor@louisvillereview.org.

The Louisville Review Corp.
1436 St. James Court #1
Louisville, Kentucky 40208

This issue: $10 ppd
Sample copy: $5 ppd
Subscriptions: One year, $18; two years, $36; three years, $54 plus $2 shipping.
Subscribers outside the United States please add $35/year for shipping.

Text and cover printed in the United States. Cover design by Jonathan Weinert. Cover artwork, *Table For . . .* , Joyce Garner, oil on canvas, 72 x 58 inches.

The Kentucky Arts Council, the state arts agency, provides American Rescue Plan funds to The Louisville Review Corporation with federal funding from the National Endowment of the Arts. *The Louisville Review* is a not-for-profit publication.

The Louisville Review Corporation is a member of the Community of Literary Magazines and Presses.

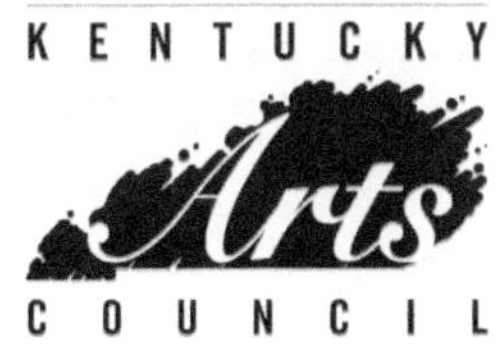

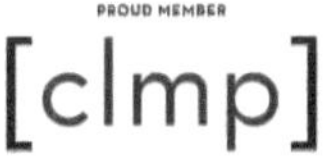

With the last few issues of *The Louisville Review*, as well as this one, *TLR* has instituted the practice of featuring the artwork of contemporary artists on its cover. This cover features a work titled *Table For . . .* by Joyce Garner, a Louisville artist who has two galleries here. On this cover, note the varieties of ages welcome at Joyce's table, as well as their various interests. And be sure to read Joyce's own note about her work, often of gigantic proportions and outstanding inclusiveness. (We're sorry our cover is necessarily small; we hope you'll visit one of her galleries here to experience the amazing size and scope of her work.)

In this issue of *TLR*, we have arranged the fiction section to spotlight the progressive ages of the various protagonists, ranging from young children, placed first, to ever older protagonists. All kinds of folks and ages are also welcome in our pages, as in Joyce's inclusive paintings.

As some of you may have noticed, after forty-five years of publishing, supported by higher educational institutions, *The Louisville Review* is now an independent institution, housed at my home, 1436 St. James Court, Louisville, KY 40208. There is a ghost here. That of poet Madison Cawein, who lived here about 110 years ago. Little known, that poet. But he did publish one of his poems in a mag almost certainly read by T.S. Eliot; Cawein's poem had images in it and a phrase—waste land—which that other poet liked. It gave T.S. the title and some of the same images for his later large new poem that became the dominant poem in English of the last century: "The Waste Land."

So you see, dear Readers, it pays off to *read* small literary mags, as well as to publish in them. At least for some. And it also pays off to SUBSCRIBE to them, for many reasons, but also so that you won't miss out on some important trigger to your own imagination. *We*, in Louisville, are eternally grateful to those of you who submit your work *and* to those who subscribe for a year's worth, or more, of fresh writing. As we invite various guest editors, we're quite unpredictable about what kind of writing, representing many moods and ideas, may appear at our table.

I want to begin by thanking Jonathan Weinert, a splendid poet himself and the author of a just-completed new autobiographical work, for serving as guest Poetry Editor for *TLR* No. 91.

Jonathan Weinert is the author of three books of poems: *A Slow Green Sleep* (2021), winner of the Saturnalia Books Editors Prize; *In the Mode of Disappearance* (2008), winner of the Nightboat Poetry Prize; and *Thirteen Small Apostrophes* (2012), a chapbook. He is co-editor of and contributor to *Until Everything Is Continuous Again: American Poets on the Recent Work of W. S. Merwin* (2012). Jonathan lives in Stow, Massachusetts.

A big thank you also to guest Fiction Editor Beth Ann Bauman, who selected the fiction for this issue along with myself and Associate Editor Flora K. Schildknecht.

Beth Ann Bauman is the author of a short story collection *Beautiful Girls*, and the young-adult novels *Rosie and Skate*, which was selected for the *New York Times* Editors' Choice list and Booklist's Top Ten First Novels for Youth, and *Jersey Angel*, selected by *Publishers Weekly*, *Boston Globe*, and *The Horn Book* as a best summer book. Beth has received fellowships from the Jerome Foundation and the New York Foundation for the Arts. She teaches fiction writing at NYU's School of Professional Studies and is on the Writing for Children and Young Adults faculty at Spalding University's Sena Jeter Naslund-Karen Mann Graduate School of Writing.

And many thanks to Betsy Woods, for continuing to serve as Editor of our Cornerstone section of poetry by writers in grades K-12.

—Sena Jeter Naslund, Editor

Table of Contents

Cover Art Essay

FICTION

CORNERSTONE
work by writers K-12

Joyce Garner

Cover Artist's Statement: *Table For . . .*

Helpful figures of speech: get everyone together around the table, turn the table, wait on tables, get a seat at the table, set the table, put something on the table (or take it off), table it for now, no room at the table, under the table. For years, I've worked with an allegory of a table. A painting might start by drawing a circle for the table. Then I draw some chairs—empty. Then I get to seat a person. They might be young/old, shy/extrovert, sly/unknowing, a participant or a witness, involved or oblivious or dreaming. There is no single protagonist.

The paintings are filled with hopes, regrets, and wishes—about the past and the future. They are like an ancestry chart or family tree where each choice branches onward . . . emotional dialogues. The interactions are not just within a family but with a family history, which includes society at large and our natural world.

Working big lets me paint novels rather than poems. But I'm an emotional artist rather than intellectual, and this comes out in the color.

Table For . . . is a flash of sun, a golden-hour daydream. A horse and rider fly by just before the food arrives and the guests settle. There is still so much to be decided, so much that is up in the air. This painting is about freezing that before, and gazing upon each possibility.

The power of that child, wearing the black patent leather Mary Jane shoes, continues to engage me.

Poetry

Mary Ann Samyn

Last of This; First of That

No *no no no*: mild admonition, a child
at the water's edge, but all is well, basically.
Undulations more than waves. Blue blue sky.
Passersby ask if I'm studying for college.
I am, I say, as anyone would, too much to explain,
reading Billy Collins so as to be reassured, somewhat.
At its best, that easy style breaks my heart,
but what are the options? *Everyone*
come watch this, says the boy on the dune.
And again, more urgently, about to jump.
You're a frog now: what only a sister could know.
All this goes down, as they say,
last day of summer; one-thing-after-another year.
A dragonfly putters by. This light belongs in a novel.
I know how it would go, but I can't write it.
Or choose not to, which is the same, in the end.
It's tomorrow here, but it's today where you are,
says the man, confident-like, to his phone,
ignoring the little curl of water so cute at his feet.
He's working on the Vision Statement, as promised.
I'm so glad I mostly have not given up, so there's that.
The paradox of writing is you have to know something;
you have to feel it isn't ever quite right.
A ladybug sits down beside me. *Oh, hi. Nice wings!*
Not so many beach days left for any of us, maybe.

Mary Ann Samyn

How Could You

—Fortunately, it doesn't matter,
as my father used to say, about sports and most things.
Doesn't matter much, I'd say.
I've been a little too interested in consequences, I guess.
Allowances and consequences.
You make allowances. You suffer consequences.
I underline the verbs, circle the nouns, as instructed.
It's possible I don't really know; entirely possible.
Things playing out; yet to play out.
The clock on the mantel ticks quite loudly—
doesn't bother me a bit. I listen most evenings.
If there was another life intended for me. . .
Well, I suppose not.
Should I squint into the distance now?
Pray on my knees?
I've heard that (which?) can work.
What did Bishop say? Doesn't hurt. Can't hurt.

Mary Ann Samyn

A GOOD THEFT, IN BROAD DAYLIGHT

Theme of the week. That's how it's done.
I tell my students; I want them to continue.
I've practiced French 378 days in a row
but could fall out of the habit at any time.
Third time's the charm, maybe, for Jude the Obscure,
an English rose of uncommon delicacy, etc.
I make the purchase. This is the day,
cold but sunny enough to sit out for a while.
Joy? Might not go that far, though I'm trying.
Feelings are valid but not necessarily interesting.
The news is neutral, but I take it badly anyways.
Why be like that? I ask the glossy book of how to live.
Careful, my mother would say, opening it.
Nothing makes everything better. Imagine that.

Adrian Blevins

Medical Status

As a matter of fact I did want to get way the fuck down
        to the pith at the beach. Yeah and be like bison

storming some little pre-fab ranch style thing. But there were
        savage husbands and loopy kids

and we all had laryngitis and the presidents were demons
        and the neighbors were narks—evildoers basically

with peestraw for hearts. And yeah I thought money
        could fix us (or Frank Lloyd Wright)

here in shitty America where moolah is your ticket
        if you aren't meaty making it. Yeah the mouth

like an oven in the nub of a kiln. O singe and blacken.
        O char and scald! And now just listen to me

coming at you damp and slow like a petty little thing
        with a hole in the heart alone in the dark like a horse cut up.

Adam Tavel

Portrait / Self-Portrait

First facts are dirt. I could hear it
in his voice—that filth, that obvious
unmooring. Startled, my mother
like a bad magician hid her body
behind the jamb. I crept upstairs and saw
her discomfiture, the only look she gave
the beggar I'm here to sketch—
tar-toothed, whiskered, and gaunt
beyond our screen, another consequence
of April. His overcoat splashed
like a flume ride. At five, I hated his eyes
and didn't keep them. What I remember
is wishing he'd walk back down the road
so the thin gravelly sizzle
of tires, that dark sibilance, could thump
him dead. I'm sorry, my mother croaked,
I'm sorry, closing the door. When she flung
it wide, moments later, weeping,
a bag of fresh bread from our cupboard
crinkling in her hands, and bellowed
that we had enough, her shout echoed
for the streetlights. No shoeprints. One car
backing out. This is the portrait I've come
at last to make—the sound of done tears
shuddering. The fact of my relief.

Kyle D. Craig

Poem in Which the Client Regrets Asking His Psychotherapist for Advice

If I am hearing you correctly, you're ambivalent
about the relationship. One part of you feels *y*,
another *x*, and that's why I'd invite you
to be curious about what the lemurs and box turtle
in your dream represent. I say that only because
I'm recalling your dinner last month
with Susan. The one on the wooden deck
overlooking the water – lobster, asparagus,
Pinot Grigio, crème brûlée and cappuccino
for dessert. Do you remember the anger you felt
when she told you to use the napkin to wipe
the cream from your moustache? I see your foot
has begun to bounce. You're folding your arms.
Would you like to explore that? You and I
have built an alliance that enables us to speak
openly. For instance, don't read too much into this,
but we'll need to further explore your relationship
with your mother. You'll need more than the scent
of lavender for your anxiety. And your pants
are a size too small. Earlier, when you said
the word *supposedly*, I heard a b instead of a *d*.
You don't seem to know how to use chopsticks,
or change an alternator. Everyone has picked up
on these facts. Your taste in literature, it's best
I leave that alone. At some point we might want
to talk about your wing tipped shoes and Vermont
clip suspenders, but right now my brain is searching
for the right words. What I'm trying to help you
with here is acceptance, given that the evidence
suggests your desires outpace your abilities.
I will say, also, in last week's session it was nice
to meet Susan. She seems to be in good shape.
I wonder if she is open to individual sessions.

Diamond Forde

After Five Years of Absence,
Momma Takes Care of Me While I'm Sick

I'll tell you how it started: a cat scratch on the back post
of my throat, a sniffle, a sneeze, a fever whose high-rise
demolition, all shattered glass & metaphor-swallowed,
diamonded my lungs like a car-marred stretch of road—
absence makes something beautiful of my mother
plastering slivered onion to the bottoms of my feet.
In cotton socks, I marinate, sick broth of a Vidalia's
pearlescent sweat. Momma swears the onion will blacken
with bacteria by morning, makes promises she can't keep
again. She spoons yogurt to soothe my fever-fried throat.
I smell a pasture of scallions, I fumble for spoonfuls
of macerated berries, habit of chasing sweetness, why I keep
coming back to reach for the hand that holds the flat silver
spoon like a ward—finally, the two of us close enough
to wound, if we wanted. When she tells me she will check
on me by morning, I need to believe her. Even while I dip
in the somnolent stream of fever-dreams, past optometrists
& their peeping scopes, jabbering cows, & a runaway
Volvo, I will weasel my feet back & forth in my socks,
a pendulum hoping the onion will drink up the dark.

Diamond Forde

Aubade

I have made book of your body, read
in your heavy lids the hooded font of sleep,
made, even, punctuation—your ticks
accenting your anxiety like apostrophes.

I'm sorry I read you, but I need to sidestep
the language your body rings—its emotions
all bells clanging in my mind's cathedral
what might soon become

danger, or a tongue-torched anger—balled
fist, tight-knit jaw, or a murkiness crawled
behind the half-drawn valance of the eyes,
this study, this habit, what my therapist calls

a survival mechanism, after four years learning
a mother could machine-gun the thinness
of my sheet metal peace. At least this means,
I've survived. At least, this means

when the sun dispatches bullets
through my curtain, I will be holy
& wholly breathing. I will mirror,
the glassy stillness of an October dawn

before cars split their beams through its glint
& if I could just hold the autumn in
do you think I could be beautiful? because
when I'm angry, I Shar Pei in a quiet rage,

& when I'm sad, my lips plump
& droop like plums, at least this means
there's sweetness still—& together
we might mechanic with any tool clanking

on my belt because we love us some me,
or least, I believe I can believe you
when you tell me you want to see
my face damned with morning again, again

Ann Pedone

To Lie Under You Like That

That day we snuck into the dept to get my stuff and

I know it got very personal

I held your hand and took you to the third floor

Bathrooms and told you that they were the ugliest

Leaving Columbia that last time was

Very anti-capitalist and every time every time we fuck

I am more assured of my uselessness

But I am speaking to you my Beatrice

And when I text you across the Park across the East River

My phone is sonorous for you

Because I am not trying to make you mine but just want

To let my hot body sing to your hot body

And I never want to signify anything ever again

Rachel Whalen

Algos

Flat-backed on the grass
we searched for Helios.

There was nothing we could do
to stop ourselves from breaking.

In the woods the bears wept.
I offered them my orchids.

In the room you knifed the robin.
In the room I learned what a room was.

As the rotting chariot roared
you collected crabapples.

You blasted them to smithereens
as I pulled red feathers out of my mouth.

Rachel Whalen

OPERATOR: OPERATOR

Lift up, there:
the tone. No one
there, Non

is there, they say
who?
and now there's

a croak in my branches,
my finger-steeple, there are
no people

nothing around
to steady, no cure,
no railing

or anvil, just
an end and another end:
mouth to string to

trap door, leading
where? Sometimes the tunnel
isn't a tunnel. I turn

towards my dead. I'm calling
for the operator:
Operator,

place my awful
call. Does it come
from a uterus

a kidney
a set of lungs

does it come at all?
Or am I again
my own open-mouthed

son, child
of Goliath, chalk circle empty
of incantation? After I abandoned my own

heaving animal, what
did I have left to give?
What could I possibly

have left to receive?

Rachel Whalen

WHERE DOES THE BODY NON COME FROM WHERE DO THEY GO

A rabbit pulled from a rabbit
minus the rabbit, Body Non accepts their math

and wants to know about body not non
they care about material, what's

at stake. They never trust the urgency
of division, the sport of words – after all

they know best that nothing
comes from nothing

and body comes from body, which requires food
and peace of mind. Body Non comes from deep

in their throat:
Rabbit begets rabbit   Non begets Non   sometimes Non

wants to be loved as a man because sometimes
that's what they are. They laugh

their throaty laugh this need not concern you. Mr. Non wants you
to be concerned about their health, their hunger, what they have

to consume. To watch them
move through the cafeteria

bursting and
astonishing.

Kevin McLellan

Boudoir

Have you seen them? John from Tennessee, Costas from Thessaloniki, and myself at those ages when I knew them.

When my heart becomes so tired of its brain that it vacates the body.

It's not the fault of the moon or of candles. They are not unalike. We are not unalike, but the others cannot know.

I read somewhere that the French have a healthy relationship with sex. Perhaps it is more about inhabiting one's own body enough so that it makes room for another? Maybe I made this up.

The window that has been closed for months is open. The dust particles circle, seemingly synchronized with one another. A razor of light cuts through the space between the curtains and window.

Those who think they know me don't. I am not a mystic, philosopher, member of any clergy, detective, psychologist, or therapist.

My brain becomes tired of its heart.

I land on the bed as I wake. Sleet pings the windows. I turn over, face the dormant flowers repeating on the wallpaper. Pillows are formidable. My favorite pillow is starting to enter its yellow period. Art is too infrequently *blanche.*

Kevin McLellan

Blue

after the Derek Jarman film

When I look into, not at, the screen—
the blinking red and green

pixels frantic behind blue, but I
can't walk too long behind this sky—

notice the exit sign and the left side
of flickering faces. I must return

to where you sit, once sat,
behind blue. The textured collage

of sounds a way to make sense
of, what you call, 'abnormal thoughts'

and I feel a heartbeat in the eyes—
a throbbing experience

onto the screen. I must shut them
again. A second hand and the hour

bells sound simultaneously, continue
as you say, *The earth is dying and we don't*

notice it. Then the sound of rain.
You mention delphiniums once more.

Kevin McLellan

James Schuyler to John Ashbery

in memory of Karl Tierney

We are tentative.
We are tentatively looking.
Landscapes unknown.
We are tentatively looking for landscapes unknown to us.
Our window.
Our window is a square.
Our window is a beautiful unlatched square picture window
          and we are tentatively looking.
Our window is ours, not the powers' that be
          and is beautiful and unlatched
          and we are beautiful and not unlatched
          and we are tentatively looking
          and do not feel a bit disturbed or troubled.
We have the light on
          and then do not.
First we have the light on, for the people
 and then we have it off, for ourselves.
No, ourselves is a lie
          for there is always darkness.
We have the direction of darkness
          so ourselves is a lie
          when we have the light on.
In the darkness is your yellow cardigan
          and our window is a square.
A square. Yes, a square
          and your yellow cardigan is in the darkness
          from your beautiful unlatched square picture window.
Your yellow cardigan is shrouding
          for we are tentatively looking
          towards landscapes that do not
          give us any indication of the other.
Tentatively, yes, tentatively looking we are
          in a beautiful square picture window

but neither unlatched nor green
    nor very distracted or troubled, really.
We are merely tentative
    and can be seen with the light on
    in the direction of darkness.

Christopher Howell

Poem for My Father on Veterans Day

If I wake in the night
and open the door
of what I suppose is that grey
house where almost nothing
has been broken since the war
or one of the wars
in which human pride and
trouble and rage
were made manifest, again,
and purified by the frank
absence of war's necessity,
what truth could I send back
to my father,
dead these twenty-five years?
My father who knows already
that most of the world's
contention comes to nothing.
How could I bring myself
to wake him
out there in his boat, fishing
his silent happiness, time
having loosened its suspenders
and left him peaceful
as wind that barely stirs cattails
along the reedy shore.
And what a shore, now, since
anything is possible
in the house of longing and
memory I build plank by plank,
the whole of it turning vaguely
as it passes under a bridge,
one light glimmering in a window,
tired looking angels asleep

on the roof, demons and sorrows
asleep outside in the snow.

Roy Bentley

OHIO

for Matt & Scott & Cait & Eoin & Erinn

As Ohioans, we know we should be wide-smiling to
and from the Kroger, grinning at the lie it can't be

any kind of an apocalypse if they deliver groceries.
I was here for the Kent State shootings. Meaning

that I was alive in 1970 and that I can remember
the day of the week the song "Ohio" was released

and made a lot of young people proud to be whose
brother or sister they were and to be living among

those willing to be shot dead or, worse, paralyzed
to stop a war. Take the song and its set of truths

in the service of all of us seeing Ohio more clearly—
as more than whites with long hair and short dresses

kneeling over the wounded and dead, Black women
and Black men in rainbow tie-dye and bellbottoms—

all that showroom-polished star-bright Newness.
All that promise based on keeping your promises.

Seriously, between you and me and the souls of the
dead at Kent State—we stole whatever we wrung

from every Firebird, every ounce of beautiful life
America lies it came by as honestly as you can.

Gabriel Welsh

Blood Pressure

It's hard to resist jumping
in the fray, isn't it? To wake up
every morning feeling like screaming
yourself to exhaustion. You work
with a guy who likes to say
the truth is and it's always
the truth for his expedience.
We want a world as easy as that—
make a pissy statement that jerks
your furry pet of truth toward you.
Lupé came here with her Mennonite
husband, who digs fracking wells
near the ridges where once they mined
dirty coal in its unrehabilitated pre-clean
splendor, when black lung was the only
consequence, and one oligarchs could shrug
more easily—the ridges where the broadband
never reaches and the only radio is Rush
and Jesus and even they break apart. Truth
wrestles with time here—the hills
once were stripped of trees,
during the years Pennsylvania
was a frontier, the railroad was yet
to cut through, steel yet a dream of iron,
and somewhere tenements boiled as grim
as the genocide dreams of an impotent
dictator wannabe, that pure product
of a nation impure in everything.
His broken fortune was still
in the growing stage, before falter,
before he awakened power he didn't know
he had, before the daily moment
when eyes part and the lungs fill
and your voice wants to lunge into the air
and your teeth know only bite.

Clay Cantrell

An Angel Walked with Me Today

I don't usually think too much
but I am superstitious, my dog feels
dejected, the weatherman is calling
for ten inches of rain by midnight.
I ignore erosion until a hollow
longing hits me. A scent of sinkhole.
I don't usually pray but pressure
grows and I fear myself, lightning-
struck, keeling over in this economy,
hot as cornbread in rain.
Dear god. What a long, strange
scent of love. Or strike dead
some deserving oak. The dog
gets skittish during storms.
Today, no shelter. Truck brakes
in the distance. The drops slap
the sidewalk like hot tears.
I picture a lexicon, a big wilting
raincoat, a blue longhouse.
She and I are extremely unlucky.
I wonder about forgiveness.
A neighbor falls in step, holding
a fistful of ash. She walks us home.
She hides us underground among
the scathed thorns and my faith
is lightly restored. Still, I resent
the free market, its dejected souring.
My dog won't die today, I won't leave
her, unlike her teeth. There are angels
among us, they say, ready
to enrich anything.

James Hejna

THE SHARD

A skilled hand dipped a brush in glaze,
and with no discernible hesitation
painted a floral pattern on a bisque vase,

an intricate trace of improvisation,
entwined stems, oblate leaves, and filled space
inclined in a rightward direction.

No one living knows his face.
A sudden tremor and an eruption
finished the man, and fired his base.

Rolly Kent

Could a Snake Be a Man?

Once, after she left New Pascua, Heather
told me that her ex-husband, the chief
of all the Yaquis, didn't need a phone to
receive word of his people on the Rio Yaqui
in Sonora. He simply watched the ants.

She introduced me to him, at least in
his human form—because, Heather said, Anselmo
could shape-shift. The time I was cornered
by a rattler on Heather's patio
she came out and screamed for Anselmo to leave.
It was the *Sabado de Gloria*,
the Saturday after Christ's crucifixion,
also the day when the walls between
the living and the dead soften and yield to
the same wishes that commanded Jesus
to walk from the tomb. I went to Heather's.

So did the huge rattlesnake, in full
afternoon sun, hunting. Could a snake be
a man? The sound of Easter rattles that shook
the square in New Pascua sent me up a ladder
onto Heather's roof. What was in the snake's
mind, if I believe her, was Anselmo,
warning her she could leave Yaqui but
it would never leave her alone. She'd always be
torn between two places. What can you do
with knowledge like that—either ignore it
or live as if a snake can be a man.

Heather heard me holler and came to the door.
There was the big snake blocking her way,
but when she saw who it was she hurled

curse after curse at Anselmo, Heather went
right up to the snake because they had
been in love once, but now it was over.

"Who knows?" Anselmo said to me before
I met him as a snake. "All kinds of change
is possible in the Creator's mind.
Nothing's ever finished. Even you.
Maybe you were one of us." He would ask
his dead mother the next time they talked.
She would know. He was sitting in the parlor
of an ordinary house, twirling some ice
in a glass. With outsiders he didn't have to be
a thousand percent Yaqui. He could take part
in the sister-and-brother-hood of light
visible at night in the stars: the silver ants
of the Creator's mind, carrying back
and forth the work of endless reunion.

Alamgir Hashmi

PTARMIGAN! PTARMIGAN!

I last saw it preening as a blueberry
patch some other place, and gosh,
here it is now, this one,
amid trees of heaven,

riotous red hemlock, larch and fir.
Whisper spruce, and with hisses,
low whistles and clucks, the leaves
stir uneasy, so I can tell the feather,

chest spot, or band from the rest.
Foraging far in the pine country—
needles after green shoots—it has altered
again, melting into the landscape;

shelters easy with flamboyant sumac,
letting in the fast underbrush, loud spice.
Lush mountainside, seeds, berries, lake
waters fill this dusky hornbeak

no matter the brownish desert kin
daily bathes in the dust. And in the park today,
looking up into treetops, I may have
overstepped the peace, tubers

or dry branches crackling everywhere.
So it looks out of red eyes, sore—
sideways of its nervous coat
of shifting colors,

scampers on the touchy ground,
wings spread out once, twice, clapped shut,
and readies to take the forest along
crazy brusque in flight.

Jack Ridl

It Could Be

On the last day of the world (a Tuesday)
I'm sitting on an old Adirondack during
a deluge of a thunderstorm. A car drives

by, the water on the street splashing
with each revolution of its tires. The world
too is turning. I know that. It always has.

No slower, no more immediate today.
It's common as air to see an angel perched
up on the corner street light. She—it is she—

lets the rain soak into her lucent skin.
Yes, she's naked, but not as you think.
Odd, however, is that I see her wings

let the rain roll across the perfect overlap
of her feathers. She's more like all the birds—
chickadees, junkos, nuthatches, cardinals,

finches that have come to the feeders
hanging from the curly willow a few feet
from our front steps. They are all here

again today. Last night I filled the feeder
just before bed. They usually empty it
in two days. It felt good—and right—

to fill those feeders. We were many
times told this day would arrive.
Those who could have stopped it

didn't. The rain has become a gullet fall,
no wind. Another car has driven by. I'm glad
I have my coffee and maybe a new book to read.

Don Bogen

A Call

> *Krähe, wunderliches Tier*
> —Winterreise

Black wings, black stick-legs, black beak, black eye
The monochrome of their variegated parts can dazzle
All shining in different ways
Transfiguring the light as if they'd swallowed it
In groups they blot out the sun
Or drift, a flotilla of black sails, across clouds
Crow—the name's a pale echo of what they shout
In a language we're unable to share

When I came back to that lovely campus after years away
They'd displaced the jay from the eucalyptus grove
His shriek thin and irrelevant in the smother of their caws
His little crest fragile as an apostrophe
Nothing stays fixed—their place is wherever they decide
Fighting over a dead squirrel on the asphalt
They lift reluctantly just before a car comes
To drop down the moment it's gone

Loss is their sustenance
Keen, stark, efficient, and quick
They hide things, dissemble, and make tools
In clucks, cackles, and long broad calls
They remember and remind
Not a bit of light escapes their notice
Their focus shameless and outside time
They will follow the dying lover in the song cycle to the end

Now they perch and wait on the sycamore limb near my window
Keeping a lookout on something I can't see
I know what's coming but they'll spot it first
Crows, crows—in your dark immediacy

Keep me from the lassitude of slow sorrow
Sharpen my blurry eyes
On whatever journey I'll find someday I've taken
Point me toward the gleaming you devour

Don Bogen

INTERLUDE

This is our life, I thought: these stairs,
you humming on your way down them
as I come up, our son's quick wave and shout good-bye
at the back door, everything
a single motion carried on the stream of time.

I could feel the fluidity of the pen as I broke
from reading about a river and its voices
to follow out on paper what I heard and had heard
and hoped to keep on hearing a long time.

And two years later when I couldn't hear it,
the stairs empty both up and down, the back door shut,
I began to hate and fear anything having to do with time.

I began to think of the past as an illusion of time
even as it drowned me in wave after wave of detail,
and I could just barely keep my head above the flow.

You were alive again in details but only in details,
like an object cluttering almost any stair of memory,
different on each step yet unchanging:
a gnarled twig, a cup, a paper boat once, ready for the flow.

Though I can hear bird song now, a wind chime you knew,
even, I imagine, this ballpoint marking the page,
the past, vivid as it is, stays silent—
no waves of air to carry a voice across the glass wall
into the endlessly shifting moment of life in flow.

Michael Mark

AFTER THE FUNERAL

We rise, off balance,
as though we've been
sitting a lifetime,

as though we've been away
from our bodies, and go
looking for our coats.

It's when they search
for theirs, too, we know
what's coming.

At the door, we pause,
maybe mention the weather
before taking a half step over
the threshold.

This is when they take the same
half step behind us.

So we stop, to relive
the stroke, the accident, years
of disease.

This is when they touch
their faces for proof
and can't.

This is when they reach
to ours.

We stand at the door, waiting
for them to let us go.

It's getting late, it's getting cold,
the traffic.

Fiction

Jane Ogburn Dorfman

Lost at the Circus

We sat up high, as we did every year for the Shriners Ringling Brothers-Barnum & Bailey Circus. It was at New Orleans' grandest auditorium, as big as a football stadium, where the Mardi Gras balls were held. Wooden flip down seats with scratchy red velvet in rows all the way to the ceiling.

When intermission came, and everybody got up to stand in long lines for the bathroom, I wanted a circus balloon. They were such balloons, wonders, a pastel balloon shaped like a mouse's head inside a huge clear one, overfilled with helium, pulling on their strings. My mother had refused last year when I was seven.

"No balloons. Too hard to get home on the bus, waste of money. You'll lose it." Indeed, already ten or twelve balloons danced on the domed ceiling. I had formulated a theory about the circus employing marksmen to shoot them down between shows. I was working on why the fancy gilded molding remained undamaged.

This year, I had money hidden in my pocket from my grandmother, and I would carry the balloon home on my lap. I pushed ahead of my mother, squeezed into some child-size gap between adults. She must have momentarily relaxed her usual death grip on my hand.

When I stopped at the hallway and looked around, I was alone, a heady feeling, I might have called out. A vigilant red-vested program seller asked if I was lost. I squeezed out a yes. He took me all the way down to the ground floor, where the three rings were. He delivered me to a woman in a nurse's uniform who presided over the Lost Child area. She sat me on a bench near the entrance to the backstage. My mother and I never sat this close. The floor was actually covered with sawdust, I could smell the wood. The workmen tightened equipment, brought out new edges to the rings. I had been crying, but I stopped.

The lost child bench was positioned right by the opening in the red velvet curtain where performers entered. There stood a girl about my age, but shorter, in a glimmering silver leotard. Her eyelids were painted vivid green and she had on lipstick. Her hair was coiled in a dark knot with a silver beaded spangle that caught the lights. I was close enough to see every comb line in her hair. The girl walked on her toes, flexed her shoulders, and bent her neck from side to side. Her skin was olive and chalk dusted her hands and arms all the way to the elbows and her legs up to the knees. I was a thin, gangly child, this girl had muscles. The chalk articulated every line in her calves and thighs. My legs were straight sticks, her knees pinched hers in.

She gave me a quick glance and a nod before she started practicing her prance. As she lifted each knee, her foot turned slightly at the ankle with the toes fiercely pointed. I got so caught up in the sight of her I could feel my own foot lifting and my toes pointing in my Mary Janes. She was one of the flyers. In a moment, I noticed the whole glittering troupe waiting to go on. They were similarly dressed, a beautiful woman in a silver leotard with light dancing off her headdress and two men in silver suspendered tights and no shirts.

What if my mother never found me, and how could she in this sea of people? I would join the troupe. I'd be left on the bench when the clowns came around with push brooms to clean up the sawdust. "What shall we do with this one?"

The girl, or maybe her mother, would speak up, "We'll take her. She needs a lot of work, but she'll fit in." I would be welcomed as a sister. I spared only a tiny thought for my mother.

But my mother did find me. Probably an announcement about a lost little girl sent her running down the stairs. She was crying with relief, I from remorse and regret.

She insisted we go right home, not from anger, I am sure she blamed only herself, but she had been so frightened she felt the need to flee. Had someone not brought her a paper cup of lemonade and a tissue we would have left then. But by the time she had finished her lemonade, the house lights were dimming. Intermission was over. We were still on the bench, ringside seats, the expensive seats, indeed in front of the people who had paid for them.

It was time for my friend's family to perform.

They walked out waving, arms stretched high, each now wore a silver cape clasped at the throat. I wiggled my hand away from my mother's to applaud. At the bottom of a shining tall ladder they paused, all turned around once more and, as one, dropped their capes preparing to ascend. Two small boys in silver ran forward to collect the capes.

A man with huge shoulders climbed up first, checking the wires on his way up. He got to the tiny platform up near the ceiling and gave it a little shake and nodded yes. The woman and the second more slender man climbed up. Then a thick white rope slid down, the girl grabbed one loop, put her foot in another and rose into the air, one hand gracefully held over her head, with applause just for her.

The trapezes were untied; one of the adults took a trial swing and landed on the far platform. The big man swung out, his hands gripping the bar, and then switched to his knees, his legs coiled in the supporting ropes. The woman went next, swinging harder and harder till she threw herself off and into his waiting hands. The younger man followed on his swing. They traded swings, flew head over heels, and took twists in the air. I could see clouds of chalk and hear the smack of their hands when they met. All this while smiling, giving an air of ease, relaxed, in their element.

Finally, the girl stepped to the edge of the platform with her toes curled tightly on the very edge. The slender man swung closer and closer, she held out her arms, he clasped her forearms, and she was in the air, carried across the space, toes pointed, her body in a v shape. She was caught by the other man on his swing then placed on the far platform. She was never flung. She was handed off with such care from one set of hands to another, hugged on each platform, never out of contact with her family. There was the feeling of flying, but no danger. Who could care about a helium balloon just rising on a string when here was real flight?

The crowd gasped and sighed. There were more tricks from the adults, catching two at a time, the man's arms bulging, but I could not take my eyes off the girl. She used a hooked pole to being the swing closer, handed the chalk bag to the woman. Then the adults dropped, one at a time, into the net and somersaulted out. The girl came down last, the other flyers holding the net on each side. She bounced on her back and then to her feet. The big man lifted her out of the net. Many bows, more waving.

I wanted her to look at me, but even at eight, I knew that was too much to expect, so I played a game that she came over, pulled the spangle from her hair and gave it to me for a keepsake as she passed. I folded my hand around it, and when my mother wanted to take that hand as we rose to our feet during the clown act I was surprised the sparkling ornament wasn't there.

We climbed all the way back up to our seats for the rest of second half. My mother got much sympathy from the other parents around us. I got mean looks for worrying my mother so much, I cried some more.

I might have seen the big cats, and maybe horses, but I was so worn out I had to be woken up to go home.

We took three different buses and then a long walk to get back to the room we shared at my grandparent's house, but my circus family—they left in the morning and went back on the road.

Sometimes, even now, I put myself to sleep imagining my other life. The girl and I grow up together; we do each other's hair and wear matching costumes. We drive the family truck from town to town and fold the nets. The family says they don't know what they'd do without me. I learn to fly.

Dennis Hurley

The Barn Swallow

Jack reached into the cookie jar and pulled out four oatmeal cookies and handed two to Martin. They stood in the cold darkness and breathed in the rich aroma of cookies and of the earth on their work jeans as they ate. "Good breakfast food, eh Bud?"

Ten-year-old Martin nodded, his mouth full. They washed the cookies down with well water, and the earth smells followed them out of the kitchen door and along the path to the barn. Early May, Martin thought, and still cold enough to see your breath in the morning darkness. He felt his uncle's hand on his neck, let it rest there for a minute steering him along, and then, impatient, he slipped free and started to run. "Last one to the barn's a rotten egg," he yelled.

Jack gave him a head start, and then sprinted up to him, ran along easily at Martin's side until they were almost to the barn and then stepped ahead. "What's that smell? Whooee. That's rotten egg, for sure." Jack laughed and unlatched the barn door. The same ritual for most of the past year, and it always ended the same, but despite his mounting losses, Martin never felt disappointed in the outcome.

Once in the barn they went about their separate chores, Jack setting up the milking machine as Martin doled out the portions of ground corn and soy and molasses to the small mixed herd of Holsteins, Guernseys and one, old, one-horned Jersey. The cobwebbed barn radio crackled with an Andrews Sisters' song just barely audible over the sounds of cows eating and the sucking-hissing of the milking machine. The morning farm report would come on next and then the part that Martin dreaded, the news. They would have to listen to the reports of the war and the battles that swept back and forth across Europe. It had been over a year since Martin's father had died in the Ardennes, over a year since his mother had fallen apart and he had come to the farm with his uncle. Over a year and still he felt the pain of it every time the news came on.

Martin stood and watched his uncle work over each cow, washing the udder and examining the bag for cuts, drawing a couple of sharp streams of steaming milk to check for infection and then sliding the cups of the milking machine into place and moving on to another cow. Sometimes Martin would watch, and ask questions, and sometimes he would just watch the barn swallows darting in and out of their nests, mud-daub barnacles on the sides of the whitewashed beams. He loved to stand in the door at sunrise or sunset and watch them as they wove their way about the barnyard, searching out flying insects and with unfailing accuracy sweeping them from the sky. Usually, the swallows were gone for only a few minutes before they darted back in and deposited their catch into the waiting gullets of their young, but sometimes they arced out over the fields and were gone for long periods of time. The loud cries of the babies made him nervous, and only after the adults came back did he feel better.

More than anything though he loved to be where he could see his uncle working. He watched him now press his thick, black hair against the jersey's flank, her tail pinned in the crook of his knee as he squatted to strip out the last of the milk by hand into the half-covered stainless-steel bucket. His brown, vein-knotted hands kept up a steady rhythm sending the milk hissing against the bucket side. Occasionally, Jack would send a quick stream toward the boy just to see if he was alert, and they would laugh together at their little game in the warm, quiet of the barn.

Martin squatted at the edge of the gutter and stared across at his uncle. "Uncle Jack." He hesitated, and Jack turned his head to look at him all the while keeping up the steady rhythm of the milking. "Are you going to join up?"

"Join up? You mean am I going to go into the army?"

Martin nodded. He stared intently at the straw under the milk pail.

His uncle gave two last pulls, stripping out the final bit of milk and stood up. "Naw, I don't guess so. I got a full-time job here."

Martin looked up at him. "You mean running the farm?"

"Heck no. That part's a piece of cake. I mean raising you." He smiled and reached out to tousle Martin's hair, but the boy ducked laughing out of the way.

When the milking was done and the milk strained into twenty-five-gallon cans and sunk in the cold water of the milk house, they released the cattle from their stanchions and drove them out into the morning light. They moved them toward the lane and Jack and Martin followed along as the herd ambled to its morning pasture. Within a few steps, the dew-beaded grass soaked their boots and made their socks clammy inside their boots. Martin whipped stones at fence posts and ran after strays that started to break up the herd. Just as they crested a rise that overlooked the mill pond, Jack grabbed Martin's arm and pointed skyward. A swooping mass of barn swallows soared and curved across the sky, and then one by one broke off and disappeared toward the barn.

"Pretty, ain't they? I love to watch them fly so free and wild like that," his uncle said. They stood and watched for a while longer, then moved the cattle the final hundred yards to the day's pasture and closed the gate after them.

Together they made and ate their breakfast of oatmeal and toast and talked over the day's work plans. It made Martin feel like an adult to have his uncle discuss what they were going to do, sometimes even asking what he thought, like his opinion mattered.

"After you finish up that toast, we're going to head out to the silo. I didn't get enough time in the fall to take down the filler tube for the silage blower. You've seen it out there haven't you, Bud? It's rusted pretty bad, and if we don't get a coat of paint on it now, it's going to rust through and won't be worth a tinker's damn when we try to blow that first cutting of alfalfa into the silo."

Martin had seen the tube hanging over the silo's edge forty feet above the ground, but he'd never thought about how it got there. Even now he didn't see how it could be brought down, but he felt excitement at the thought of it.

After they washed the dishes, they made their way out to the barn again. Jack stopped at the machine shed first for some wrenches and a coil of rope. When they got to the barn, he dumped the tools on the ground outside the door and they went around to the back where the silo rose straight up along the side of the barn, its wood sides just catching the sun, holding it for a moment and letting it slide around the curve and off over the barn roof. The blower tube stood alongside like a thin, mirror image of the silo itself, rising up until the hooded cap disappeared over the top edge.

"Now what we're going to do," his uncle said, "is take this thing apart and lower it to the ground." He stopped and looked up at the top of the silo. "I'm going up inside and take that cap off and put it on the rope. I'll lower it to you, and when it's on the ground, you untie the rope so's I can pull it back up and rig it to a pulley up there. You understand?"

Martin looked up at the narrow tube and then back at his uncle. He felt a dry metallic taste in his mouth, and he felt like he wanted to say something, but he didn't know what. Finally, he just nodded his head.

"And most of all you just remember to stay clear until that thing is on the ground, you hear? I don't want you getting squashed like some

June bug."

"I know, I know," Martin said. "I'll be careful."

They went around to the barn door, and he helped his uncle carry the tools and rope into the barn. Martin stood in the narrow shaft alongside the silo, its steel rod steps rising up into the shadow darkness above. The silo echoed hollowly as Uncle Jack started up, the rope around his shoulders, the wrenches stuffed into his belt. Martin stuck his head through the lowest access door and looked up toward the sky. The wooden slats which looked so tight from the outside showed small tears and holes, and the sunlight pierced the wounds and broke up into a latticework along the west side. Martin went out of the barn and around the back.

He looked up. Heavy clouds broke up the sunshine now, and they billowed and rolled across the sky and disappeared over the edge of the barn roof. The effect made Martin feel as if the silo was swaying, and he looked down to get his bearings. When he looked up again, his uncle appeared at the top. He straddled the edge of the silo and slowly inched around toward the filler tube. The boy's gaze froze on the fleck of color and movement silhouetted against the sky like some fragile bird. At this distance the figure appeared so small that it didn't seem possible that it could be Jack. He felt a strange sensation begin to burn at his insides. His palms began to sweat, and he felt himself clenching and unclenching his hands. His uncle had reached the fill tube now. Jack waved and called down to him. "How you doing, Bud?"

Martin waved back. "I'm doing OK." He got the words out, but he didn't feel any truth in them. He hoped his uncle didn't notice.

Now Jack leaned down the outside of the silo to unbolt the top section of tube. As he hung over, he supported himself by hooking one leg over the inside edge of the silo and putting one foot on the outside steel support band. He maneuvered a wrench out of his belt, put it to the first nut and strained to break it free. It wouldn't give. "Thing's rusted pretty bad already, Bud. I may have to send you back for some oil to get it to break free."

Jack repositioned himself and twisted so that he could get some leverage on the wrench. As he did, his foot slipped off the steel band and, in an instant, he was dangling by one leg, flailing out with his arms in an attempt to wrap them around the silage tube for support, the rope down over his head and shoulders, tangling his arms. Martin let out a weak cry and sank to his knees. The only sound now was the scraping of his uncle's hands on the metal tube as he tried to get a grip, his panting audible even so far away from the ground. Just as he seemed to get a firm hold with his hands, they would break loose, and he would swing down again, swaying like a limp doll along the curved wood. Finally, after what seemed hours to Martin, Jack got an arm around the tube. He held on while he worked the twisted mess of rope over his head and let it drop. It uncoiled as it fell and then reassembled itself in a series of soft thumps at the base of the silo. Free of the rope, Jack managed to push himself upright. He wrapped his arms around the hooked, metal mouth, rested his forehead against its rusty surface and clung there breathing deeply.

Tears were running freely down Martin's cheeks, and he didn't want his uncle to see him cry. He got up and ran around the corner of the barn and fell to his knees in the cool, dark shadows. He knelt there sobbing inconsolably for a minute and then his insides heaved, and he covered the ground with his partially digested breakfast. Afterwards he stood for a moment and then, shaking all over, he leaned against the rough barn siding and slid again to the ground. There he drew his knees up to his chest, buried his head in his folded arms and wept quietly.

Fifteen minutes later, his uncle stood beside him. "You okay, Bud?" Jack bent down, hands on knees to look at the boy's tear-stained face. Martin nodded, eyes closed. "Come on then. We're going to let that filler tube go for today, but that doesn't mean we're going to slack none. We've got a tractor tire to fix, so we might as well get to it." Martin looked up at his uncle's dark face against the blue backdrop of sky. A swallow darted across the space behind Jack's head, and then disappeared. "You sure you're okay, Bud?"

Martin smiled up at him. "Yep, I'm fine."

Jack took Martin's hand and pulled him up. He put his hands on the Martin's shoulders and looked him in the eye. "I'm glad you're here to work with me," he said. "You really help me a lot." Martin smiled again.

As they started for the machine shed, he felt his uncle's strong hand against his neck.

Edward Jackson

SHAVING

Your dad woke from a twelve-day coma. He was forty-seven and living in the in-between measurements of time. You were fourteen. He shared a room with four men at a nursing home that specialized in neuro diseases like Parkinson's and MS. He had the latter. During the coma, the nursing home moved him to a critical care room. A room to himself that was dim and quiet. As if he needed more rest. He'd been in a coma for almost two weeks. Confused as to how much time had passed, his mind was slow to reboot and the body lost even more mobility. Before it was a paralysis below the waist. When he woke from the in-between time, the paralysis crept up to his lower chest. They said it would eventually spread everywhere. He would need a vent to breathe soon they said. He made sure those that said these things to him understood he'd never be on a vent again after the twelve-day coma.

This new paralysis made a regular wheelchair impossible since he needed some stability to keep his body upright. This chair they put him in was different. It had a tray that all but pressed into his chest. It pushed his body to the back of the seat, kept his trunk upright. He was strapped in like a child. But it worked. They said your dad lost trunk control. Funny to think of your midbody as a trunk. The new chair, the Geri chair, was weird and bulky. He was groggy for a few days. You spent as much time as you could there waking him up. They moved him back to his room. The room with four beds was only occupied by three men now. One of his roommates had died. A blow to morale for the other three. The man that died swore a lot. He was forty-six.

You told your dad about the death of his roommate, but he interrupted you asking how many days he had been in the coma. Twelve. Twelve days. You told him. Again. And Again. He touched his twelve-day beard and scratched at it. He asked for a mirror and shook as he tried to hold it examining his face. His overgrown nails scratched his face and small spots of blood appeared. You touched his hands and put them on the tray to stop him from scratching his face.

You bit your fingernails nervously. You'd been a biter since you could remember. You scratched his face for him, slowly and left no scratches. He closed his eyes.

"Get my shaving kit out of my closet," he said. He hated beards.

                                    The Louisville Review

You pulled the bag out and turned on the electric shaver. "No, it's too long now. Go fill up that mug with hot water from the bathroom and use a safety razor."

"I'll get a nurse to find an aide to do it," you said.

"No. I want you to do it. You need to learn. Soon you'll be shaving. Might as well learn on me. You need to learn a lot of things."

"I've never . . ."

"Just go run the water till it's hot."

Even your dad interrupted you. Everyone interrupted you. People in your family interrupted each other as if time were so scarce there wasn't enough of it to listen to the end of each other's sentences. They were right. Time was running out. You did as he asked. You felt it was rude to do so otherwise even though you were scared to do this.

He directed you to shave his face. He was teaching you to shave your own.

He told you how to hold the razor upward on the neck to avoid bumps he called razor burn. The razor went downward on the cheeks. You shook at first and cut him. He directed you to use a styptic pencil that was in his shaving kit. He told you every man needed to have a styptic pencil to stop the bleeding. He educated you on the reasons why placing a cube of toilet paper on a shaving cut was stupid. He warned that doing that would result in a scab. He told you about a time he went through the day with toilet paper stuck to his face. Styptic pencils it was. There was some benefit to being under medical care for so long. He got to know and use words like styptic.

To achieve sideburns, he discussed how to hold the back of a comb for a straight line. It was the 80s after all he told you, no need for mutton chops, but might as well make use of the overgrowth for some good sideburns. He specified to hold the cheek tight with your left hand to keep the skin from slacking.

Shaving him was intimate. You'd seen your dad in uncomfortable situations due to his disease, but those times felt clinical and medical. This moment, this lesson, the shaving, it was different. It wasn't so much a dad-son bond, but an intimacy that people share when they know time is precious or running out. Guards get let down during those times, feelings too.

You examined his face and saw spots and scars you'd never noticed. He was handsome, thick black hair with some graying around the temples. He had the same five finger forehead that you and your sister had.

You wondered if she had ever examined him that closeup before. He had what he called strawberry nose. You had that too. Pores that looked like strawberry seeds if not cleaned properly. His lips were cracked from a lack of moisture due to the breathing tube that was inserted into his throat during the coma.

After shaving, you washed his face with Dial soap and a washcloth. Then he asked you to moisturize his skin. He said people like you and him never should use aftershave. There was no need for that shit with the fair and rough Irish skin you were cursed with. He told you the alcohol in aftershave would dry your skin out. Instead, he directed you to put moisturizer on his skin. Then he said you shouldn't do that yourself until puberty was over. He directed you to find his medicated Chapstick in his dresser drawer and you applied it to his chapped lips. You learned from him that all other kinds of Chapstick were bullshit and that light blue medicated was the only one that worked.

He asked you to get him a certain shirt out and discussed deodorant and what kinds to use. The goal was to avoid offensive smells like musk and cheap brands. Throughout all this you played New Order's *Substance* on the stereo you'd brought from home. He told you he liked Side 1 particularly the first song, *Ceremony*, which technically was a Joy Division song first. But you liked the New Order version better and was glad he did too. He said the sound was lovely and the words were painful. What strange words for a song to contain for a listener in the same sentence. Painful and lovely. The song felt fitting when Bernard Sumner sang *This is why events unnerve me, They find it all, a different story . . .*

You wheeled him to the dining hall and his arms were weak from a lack of use during the coma, so you fed him. He asked you if you could leave the stereo for a while, and you didn't tell him you already planned to, instead you smiled and nodded. You put a Tennessee Three album on and got your backpack and said goodbye and headed out. As you walked down the hallway you looked at the cinderblock walls painted in vibrant colors. His hall was off white with a huge emerald-green stripe painted on the middle row of cinder. You were glad it was green. It was his home now and the color of the stripe was significant in ways you couldn't explain.

On that walk down the hallway, you realized there were so many things a father teaches a son and that your father wasn't afforded the time to do this with you. His time was limited. He lived in between time and little was left. You thought of all the talks that weren't going to occur in your future. Talks about sex and love. Money and jobs. Lawn mowers and barbeques. Jump starting cars and buying stereo equipment. Suits and ties.

You thought how you used words like *I love you* to make him feel better because it was the only way you knew how to alleviate the pain of his disease. But this education of shaving he gave you was perhaps more significant than any words of affection you could say to him. This education proved you were wrong in thinking only words could give comfort. You realized that with what little time you had left, you needed to be more active in the encounters with him. Not just visiting him, spending time with him and saying *I love you.* You knew that while you could learn these lessons about being a man from uncles or others, you knew he wanted to be the one to teach you these things, and you needed to learn them from him. As you walked out of the nursing home you got on the bus to the mall where you would buy a tie. Seemed learning how to tie a tie from him was a good place to start.

John Sims Jeter

SULLY

My wife has died. You would have liked her.

Well, I'm pretty sure you would; however, she was a hard person to get to know. Even though I knew her, I still wasn't sure I really knew her.

We grew up less than a mile apart in a hilly section of northeast Alabama. At any rate, I didn't meet her until I was fourteen, and it was only in a passing way, one could say. She was eight years older than I was. Maybe I ought to start off with some background.

My ma and paw were country folk who liked square dancing, fiddle playing, making quilts, and taking a sip or two of homebrew—and stronger. I had two older sisters and when I was seven my ma had twins—a boy and a girl. The girl died when she was only two years old. My older sisters became very protective of my younger brother. They often dressed him in his twin sister's clothes and, later on, in some of their old clothes. They treated him like the girl they wished he was. I guess that didn't hurt him any because, so far, he's turning out to be the best liked and made the best grades of all us kids.

Oh, here's another note about our community. Folks used to say, ". . . we live so far out you have to pump in sunshine." Not much news filtered in and there certainly wasn't any from our community worth hearing about. To me folks were so secretive that I felt we all were closed in by a fence, with a few well guarded gates.

I finished grade school when I was thirteen. Back in those days, and in my neck of the woods, you had eight years of grade school followed by four years of high school. There was no kindergarten except one where an old neighbor woman would teach kids how to draw and how to print their ABC's and numbers—and sometimes, even how to use the restroom. Around noon time, she would give them a good meal and would follow up with a cookie and some Kool-Aid before sending them home. She did this for boys and girls, for black and white, plus any other kids who crossed her doorstep.

Like I said, there was no middle school or junior high; you went straight from grade school into high school. From the speaker at my grade school graduation, I learned that only about half the kids who lived in our communities completed grade school and that half of those who did would drop-out before finishing high school. His speech made enough of an impression on me that I promised myself I would graduate high school—and maybe beyond.

By the time I started high school I had turned fourteen—some of the older kids at the school were in their twenties. Though I was barely fourteen, I felt a little more grown up than I had at thirteen. At the start of summer, I was still thirteen and only five feet and two inches tall. Yes, quite the runt. When I enrolled at Wallace High School I was five feet and eleven inches tall, almost six feet. Yep, I grew nine inches that summer and thinned down. My back has given me problems ever since.

My family had no car, and no one to drive me to school if we did. School was about three miles away and in good weather I would walk. If it was raining or bitterly cold, or even worse, I caught the big yellow school bus

On my way to school, whether walking or on the bus, I would almost always be passed by a funny looking car. It was an old Pontiac which had no rear end to speak of. A sheet metal contraption, just behind the front bench seat, extended from the roof down to the frame. The gas tank, exhaust pipe, differential, tires, and muffler plus everything else back that way were exposed and caked with mud.

I had noticed that the driver was a youngish woman and that when I arrived at school the car, or contraption, would be sitting in the parking lot, not very far from the building. I reckoned the driver must either be a teacher or that she worked in the lunchroom.

In early October, on my way to school one day, the wind began to pick up and rustle the tree leaves as well as those piled up alongside the road. The leaves were still damp from yesterday's rain and the air had that good smell I associated with the start of high school football season. My community may have been off limits to all outside forces and events, but this was Alabama; and in Alabama, nothing keeps football out.

Boiling up over the nearby hills, I saw dark clouds—the kinds that usually precede an incoming storm, sometimes a tornado. My pace stepped up and I began jogging. A tooting horn behind me caused me to swivel my head. It revealed the welcome sight of the contraption. I moved off the gravelly road and stuck out my thumb. I had heard tales that the uplifted thumb was what hitchhikers used to flag down a ride. I hoped it would work. The car pulled up beside me and the driver motioned me in. In less than five seconds we were pelted by large drops of rain that were soon joined by hail. Pretty soon, the driver slowed down to let the wipers keep up with the downpour—they were fighting a losing battle.

The driver turned and drove over a culvert and onto a dirt road that led to a farm house. About five yards off the main road she stopped. "It's pretty clear in this spot and we can get a good view if a twister's coming. And there aren't trees close enough to come down on us. We'll wait and see. My name is Sully."

"Uh huh. Thanks for stopping." A good bit of rain from several places entered into our front seat cave. "I'm Brick."

Stillness began to fill our small space. The sky turned that shade of green it does before big windstorms. She seemed to have read my mind, "Could be a twister, you smell that sulfur?"

"Yes, I do." For a second I fell silent. "I've seen your car at school. Are you a teacher?"

"No. I'm a student. Matter of fact, I'm a senior this year. Your name, Brick, is a bit unusual."

"Uh huh. I was named after my grandpa—kinda. He was a brick mason."

"My mother's father was named Sullivan."

We exchanged a few more nothings before Sully said, "Looks like the worst weather has moved on." She started the car, crossed the culvert over the ditch, and slid back onto the road. The ditch had become pretty nearly filled with water but was still several inches below the road level. I felt safe.

When the sun peeked out a bit, we exchanged some murmurings about the weather and other stuff. Some cows were coming out from under the trees. I looked down and glanced toward Sully's feet and the pedals. I suddenly realized she was working both pedals with one foot

She must have sensed my gaze and said matter-of-factly, "I only have my left leg."

I was embarrassed that she had sensed my stare, and I only added to my embarrassment. "What happened to the other one?"

"I left it in Viet Nam."

She pulled into her customary parking place. "Well. Have a good day."

"You, too."

The school year was nearing late May. I still walked to school on good days and caught the bus if the weather was bad. When I was walking, the contraption would give me a horn toot as it passed by.

One day, it stopped right next to me. Sully waved to me, "If you want a ride, just jump on in."

I opened the door, "Thanks, Sully."

We rode in silence but as we neared the school, she asked, "Would you like to take me to the school dance?"

My heart jumped into my throat and I could only nod a silent 'yes' answer.

"Nobody's asked me to go, and you don't have to. It's okay if you'd rather not."

"I would really like to—but I can't dance."

"Me neither. But I used to."

We reached the parking lot and went our separate ways.

The next morning, I was dawdling along on my walk to school. I was hoping Sully would stop and we would have time to talk. My hopes were answered as she stopped and motioned me to climb on in.

She told me the time and day of the dance and that it would be held in the school gym. "If it's all right, I can pick you up at your house."

"We live up on Post Ridge Road. I'll stand out by the mailbox waiting for you."

"Will it be okay with your folks?"

"They won't care. I'll just tell 'em I'm going to the school dance."

"You sure it's okay?"

"Paw will be out drinking and Ma will be at her sister's working on a quilt. I got a younger brother but he stays with my sisters on Saturday and Sunday. They're both married and live over near Steele."

Dance day arrived and Sully picked me up as I stood near the mailbox. The contraption had received a washing and most of the mud was gone from the frame. The wall of sheet metal, however, was as rusty as ever.

The interior smelled nice and had been spiffed up. "Would you like to drive, Brick."

"You better, I don't have my license." I didn't mention that I wasn't old enough. I really could drive a little—and most everyone I knew drove tractors and other farm stuff.

"Well, hang on, here we go." She revved up the engine and welcome breezes blew in on us to replace the still and humid evening air. "That feels good." Sully fed the contraption more gas and threw her head back in a laugh. She zoomed past the school and onto a paved highway.

"Let's see what Old Lizzie can do." The contraption jumped forward and I stuck my arm out the window. Did I mention that Sully called the contraption 'Old Lizzie?'

She drove at least three miles down the highway. Just past a motel, she made a U-turn. "Better head back. Don't want to miss the dance."

Sully's long-skirted dress clung tightly to her body. I had hardly ever seen her walk; but she and her crutch moved with ease. We sat down at a table for two—where the snacks were already in place. I got up and bought a Coke for each of us. I heard several whispers: "Look! There's that girl with one leg." "Girl heck, she's old enough to be my mother." I pretended not to hear.

I did not see anyone from my class, that is, freshmen, in the half-filled gym.

The disc jockey played a slow piece. Although I couldn't dance, I said, "Let's dance, Sully."

She gave me a quizzical look.

"Just put your foot on top of one of mine. We'll just move around—nothin' fancy like them other kids been doing."

She nodded, "Okay."

When *In the Still of the Night* spun out, she nodded, "Thanks. That was fun." We sat down in silence before she added, "I haven't danced since I was eighteen." There was a long pause. "Then I went off to war—to help with the medical supply groups."

Over the next hour, or so, we danced a couple of more times. When we sat at our table we mostly hummed, or sang along, with the music. "You want another Coke—or anything else?"

"Thanks, but no. I think we oughta head home."

When we pulled up alongside our mailbox, she turned off the engine. "Thanks, Brick. I had a real good time." I went to open my door but froze when she asked, "Could I give you a kiss?"

As I pulled the door shut, I slid down the bench seat to be nearer to her. I felt I could pucker up okay, but should I close my eyes? I decided to do so as our lips drew closer. It wasn't exactly what I had anticipated, but I didn't want to hold on too long. My tongue eased through my lips as we separated. Sully simply said, "Thank you."

I opened my door and was about to get out when she said, "Just a second, I have something to tell you." Was she about to criticize my kiss? "Thanks for taking me to the dance—and for the dances." She paused. "Tomorrow, I'm going to Tuscaloosa to study nursing. The GI Bill will pay for it. It's a three year course. I can write, if it's okay with you—and I'll let you know when I'm back this way." She spoke so fast I didn't have time to butt in.

I felt very much alone. "It's okay with me." I eased out of the door. As I neared the mailbox I saw a small cluster of forget-me-nots—still holding on despite the heat. I had noticed that a lot of girls at the dance wore flowers. I picked up a fistful. "Here are some flowers for you Sully."

"Why thank you. They're forget-me-nots and I'll certainly remember you." She reached out and drew me closer to her window. She gave me a big, smacking kiss.

I didn't want to go to sleep but I guess I eventually did.

I did hear from her over the next three years and on a few occasions when she was home we went to the Creamy Dairy in Oneonta for ice cream. On our last trip, or date as we called it, I drove her new car. It was really another old car, but you couldn't see the mud-caked frame and it wasn't closed off with rusty metal. She asked if I wanted to take her to the school dance—this time, my school dance. "Of course." I said, "I sure do."

The day before the dance Sully drove us to Anniston to see a movie.

She picked me up on the day of the dance. I had gathered her some forget-me-nots and put them in a vase with some water. I also had a large one, along with a pin, that I pinned on her when we got to school. We pretty much repeated the same routine we had followed three years earlier when I took Sully to her dance.

On the way home, Sully said, "Why don't we go over to Tifton and get married. I've got a job in Anniston and we can work to put you through college. No need to stop with high school." I recalled the words of my grade school graduation speaker.

Tifton was a small Georgia town near the Alabama border where underage marriages, and other possible marriage-blockers, didn't matter.

I hesitated, "Tomorrow's Sunday; could we go over on Monday?"

"Actually, Monday's my first day at work. They'll marry us on Sunday."

We were married.

Sometime later, I had cooked us a fine dinner and Sully would soon be home.

I heard a muffled cry and a thud from the stairwell.

Sully died yesterday.

We were about to celebrate our one-week anniversary.

Patricia Dutt

The Low-Income Apartment

Ester Brook's bedroom shared a wall with a couple who fought. After waking up from a night of partying, they'd get ready for their low-paying, under-the-table jobs, and she'd hear chairs scrape against the floor, and the microwave beeping for attention. His voice would get louder and faster, and she'd cry: "I'll do better! Just give me a chance! I need another chance!" The fighting seemed unfair, and made Ester feel protective towards the young woman.

When she wasn't substitute teaching or taking care of her children, Ester worked in her bedroom, which was also her office. There were three children. The girls shared the other bedroom, and the boy, the youngest, slept on the couch. Still, Ester had her own room, and the room's saving grace was a giant window which overlooked the city below.

One morning while the children were seated at the kitchen counter, eating oatmeal and orange slices, Ester said: "This won't last forever." She was referring to the incessant fighting next door, and their tiny second-story apartment, one of 200, which was very different from their previous house, a stone house with the swing set near the university. Still groves of mature pines and spruces, and tall forsythia mixed with bayberry softened the landscape.

"We do this for now. Everything changes, and you might not always notice the change, but that's the way of the world. Nothing ever remains the same."

"Like birds migrating," Leah said. "They have to, to live." At twelve, she was the eldest and already considered herself a scientist.

"Right. And we all need to be flexible and patient."

"Why are they always fighting?" Leah said.

"They're trying to communicate to one another, but there are better ways to get across your point. I think fighting is just a bad habit." Ester's parents had bickered about everything, and she vowed never to inflict that on her children.

"Like biting your fingernails," Leah said.

"Farting," Paul said, and giggled. He was six.

"Sometimes you need to fart," Ester said.

"I agree with Mom," Ruth, the middle one, said.

"To break a bad habit, substitute a good one," Ester said. "Most of what we do or think is habit." She glanced at the three of them and it seemed to her that they were listening.

"Maybe for arguing you could substitute slow, quiet talk with long pauses. That kind of talking is a skill, so you'd need to catch yourself, and say, 'Oh my gosh! I just raised my voice. Bring it down,' or 'Slow it down,' because I did not give that person a chance to say what she wanted to say. It's hard to think when you're upset, when your heart is beating like a galloping horse."

Ester said a lot to her kids, and she was never sure what resonated with them. Having just moved to the East Coast, she lacked the sounding board of a close friend, and her family lived hundreds of miles away. As the kids finished their breakfast, Ester stood at the kitchen counter, spraying diluted bleach on the stove and inside the cupboards. The battle with the roaches was constant: as soon as one fell, another six took up the cause.

The arguing could go on for an hour. Still, Ester was fond of her neighbors, Jayla and Josh. A few weeks ago, they were partying with friends, and she knocked at the door and asked them to turn down the music. They surprised her by complying immediately. The next day, Jayla stopped by and apologized. Women did that, Ester thought, not men.

Before Ester divorced, her mother-in-law visited her to announce that where she came from in Europe couples did not divorce, and whatever disagreements Ester had had with her husband would pass. Ester knew differently and she braced herself for punishment. Her mother-in-law's last words to her were: *You will be a single mother living in a cramped, dirty, low-class, drug-infested apartment with three young and impressionable children. And you, Ester: you will have no friends. You will be lonely.*

Ester did find an affordable house. The backyard was mostly woods and there was a metal swing set that needed only two new seats. The children could stay in the same schools. But she couldn't afford the down payment until the marital house was sold, and Ester's ex, who still lived there, refused every single offer. There was nothing Ester could do. There were other things she had little control over. Paul, for instance, often soiled himself the night before visitations with his dad, Ruth did not laugh as much, and Leah, the most sensitive one, began scratching her face until it bled, and tormented everyone with nightly screaming fits. Once, Ester slapped her on the face, not a hard slap, but it made an impression on Leah. *The screaming stopped?* a therapist said. *It did,* Ester said. The therapist suggested Ester write a contract that stipulated an immediate and meaningful consequence; if Leah screamed for more than 10 minutes, she would get one slap. The second slap, Ester's mother had always said, is *My Anger.* Within two days, the screaming stopped.

The children were tasked with figuring out how to share the bathroom, the computer, and food decisions, so Ester introduced the tennis ball: only the possessor of the tennis ball could talk. The others had to listen.

One night after dinner, as Leah was washing the dishes and the children were playing *Chutes and Ladders*, Jayla appeared at her apartment door. "Please," she said, "we need a ride to the hospital!" Her eyes gushed with tears. Josh, who was leaning on Jayla, wheezed, his drawn face barely registering anything.

Jayla paced back and forth along the tile floor. She was not allowed in back. The lights were bright and it was cold in the empty waiting room, but a TV propped near the ceiling made the room feel more populated and purposeful.

"I really need a smoke," Jayla mumbled, her eyes wide. Her tread was heavy and slow, and she'd get to one end of the room, and she'd stop as if she was working something out, grit her teeth, then turn around and relax her face, then pace in the opposite direction. She was a tall woman with black hair that went every which way, and she carried her beige purse with her like some kind of talisman. This went on for a while. The kids looked from the TV to Jayla, then back to the TV. Jayla didn't have money for a taxi and Ester thought she could use the company, so they stayed in the emergency room.

Jayla was summoned to a lighted cubicle where a young receptionist with purple hair sat. A discussion ensued, then Jayla turned around and reported that Josh needed to be observed, that it would be a half hour or so.

"We'll wait," Ester said.

"Can we get something from the vending machine?" Leah said.

Ester gave Leah three quarters and the tennis ball, and said, "Figure out how to share." The three children stood before the vending machine with its shiny packages of cookies and candy, and Leah, jiggling the quarters in one hand. She gave the tennis ball to Ruth.

"Snickers bar," Ruth said smiling, as if this was the best thing that happened to her all week. Then she gave the ball to Paul. He pressed his index finger against the glass, indicating the M&Ms.

Leah took the ball. "The Snickers bar would be hard to divide—I don't have a knife. Those M&Ms could roll all over the place."

Jayla stopped pacing and watched them, and the bargaining went back-and-forth until they agreed on a bag of pretzels. The children sat down, and Leah counted out the pretzels into their hands. When they started arguing about which TV program to watch (there was no TV in the apartment), Jayla asked for the tennis ball, and the ball went here and there until they agreed on a re-run of a 1970s sitcom. The two girls placed themselves on either side of Jayla, while Paul curled up on Ester's lap.

Leah said suddenly: "It's not always fun at my dad's."

"Your parents are divorced?" Jayla said.

The girls nodded glumly.

Paul's eyes kept fluttering: it was nearly nine, and that was late for him.

"That sucks," Jayla said, nodding her head. "My parents never got married. I was so young. I don't even have a picture in my mind of who my dad was."

"Do you know where he lives?" Leah said, sitting up straighter, separating herself from Jayla, so she could get a better look at her.

"No, and I don't care."

Leah looked at her as if she did not believe Jayla, but at the same time, would accept her answer as if she'd run across this before and now negotiated such hurdles seamlessly. "I miss having my own bedroom, and it's not that I don't love my sister (and here Ruth smiled, like a nine-year-old smiles, with the missing two front teeth), but we had a large house with very nice views to the woods and a creek. I didn't have to take a bus to school. I don't appreciate the bus ride. The other students are not well-behaved. I would have to say they are wild."

"Once you get to know them, it might be better," Jayla said. "They might just be showing off. You know kids—most of the time they just want attention? Kids are like that. I've always lived in apartments, so I've known a lot of kids."

"You've never lived in a house?" Leah said.

"Nope. That's the way it is. With a house, you have to paint it. Put in new carpets."

"We don't walk on the carpets with our bare feet—we keep our socks on."

They watched the TV. Then Jayla got up to the use the restroom and when she came back, she looked closer at Leah, and said: "Looks like you got a spider bite on your cheek. Or did you get in a fight?"

Leah shook her head.

"Just kidding. But you do have blood on your cheek. Hold on." Jayla started digging through her beige purse. It had a plastic handle and lengthwise cracks that looked as if they could rip at any second. "Here," she said, and she handed Leah a rumpled pack of tissues.

Leah took one tissue and thanked her, then gently patted her cheek. She looked at the blood as if surprised.

"It could be a bug bite," Jayla said. "Bugs in apartments are especially hard to get rid of. A friend of mine has bed bugs. The manager already fumigated twice. It's a big deal: you have to clean the kitchen and don't leave any pots out. You have to put your shoes and coats in the closet. Anything that you leave out can get bug spray on it. Especially in the bedroom where the bed bugs live inside the mattress." She went on about the bugs, what they looked like, the splotches of blood they left on everything.

"It's not a bug bite," Leah said suddenly. She added nothing more.

Re-runs of *Charlie's Angels* appeared on TV, then *The Partridge Family*. Paul was snoring, Ruth too, her head having fallen against Jayla's shoulder.

"Are you in college?" Leah said.

"I was. I dropped out after my first year. It was too much for me, you know, to work and take classes at the same time."

"What were you going to be?"

"A nurse. I always wanted to be a nurse."

"I can see that," Leah said, as if she was a grownup, appraising Jayla's net worth for the next 30 years.

Jayla smiled. In the three months that they'd been neighbors, Ester had never seen Jayla smile. It changed her whole face, and she looked like a 20-something on her way to wow the world other than someone perched on the slick slope of poverty.

"I was just getting started, then I ran out of money. I didn't know anything about loans or grants."

"I'm going to college."

"You are?"

"I'm going to be a scientist. I'm already doing scientific studies. When I was in fourth grade, I started a *Save the Rainforest Group*. Sadly, we did not save the rainforest." Leah sighed.

"That would be a big project," Jayla said. "Let's see: four stories, right? Emergent, canopy, understory, and forest floor. That was one of my college courses. Lots of cool birds."

Leah nodded, clearly impressed. "Since fourth grade, I've been paying attention to birds." Leah's forehead wrinkled. "Wherever I go, I watch birds. My Mom gave me a bird identification book so I can identify the more common ones. I've seen an Eastern Screech owl. They go *hoo-hoooo*. Like a person saying, *Who is there?* And woodpeckers. *Rat-a-tat-tat*. I was surprised that there are so many different kinds of woodpeckers. And those tall black birds with the yellow beaks that perch on treetops? The birds near the lake? Cormorants. I used to go to the lake with my grandmother and dad. No more."

"I'm sorry," Jayla said.

"I think what surprised me is that even though the birds are so different, they all get along. Like at bird feeders: they take turns. They have to cooperate, otherwise they might die. I wish I'd brought my book with me. I would say it's my favorite book, but I don't have it on me now. We left in a bit of a hurry tonight." Leah looked serious.

"Thank you for taking me and Josh," Jayla said to Leah, and she glanced at Ester.

"It's my Mom." Then Leah said, "What's that tattoo on your arm? What does it mean?"

Jayla rolled her sleeve up to her shoulder. "This is a cat here." She pointed with a blood-red fingernail that made her skin look darker. "My cat, Sylvester."

"I know Sylvester." Leah squinted: it was hard to see the contrast of the colors against her skin.

"And this swirl of blue and gold and green? It represents a dream."

"A dream of what?"

"I don't know. Just a dream."

"Why'd you get a tattoo?"

"The tattoo says what is important to me about life. It says who I am."

"Do they last forever?" Leah said.

"I think so."

"But what happens if you change?"

Jayla looked dumbfounded.

From the TV came gunshots, screams, and calls of *Police!*

"Why would that happen?" Jayla finally said.

"Because . . . everything changes. My Mom said so. And I think my whole life changed in the past few months."

"I don't know. There's so much on my mind. That never occurred to me. I don't have time to think about stuff like that; most of the time, I'm just trying to get by."

Then everyone was quiet. Even Ester had closed her eyes.

"You know what I think?" Leah suddenly said.

"What?"

"You have a nice singing voice."

"You hear me singing?"

"We hear a lot."

"I love to sing, and I would like to sing in a band, and make some money. Be a star! I could see me doing that someday."

Leah nodded and patted her cheek with the crumpled tissue.

"Right now I sing in church," Jayla said. "The church on Cherry Street."

"I don't go to church. I might when I'm older though."

"Do you hear anything else?" Jayla said quietly.

"Sometimes we hear people fighting." Leah saw Jayla's mouth fall and sadness in her eyes, and she added quickly: "But fighting is just a habit, right? Like biting your nails. It's something you can unlearn." She shrugged as if it was a minor and rectifiable inconvenience.

Everyone was quiet again. Paul and Ruth were snoring. There was melodramatic music from the TV, and the screen was taken up by a protagonist, sweating and panting with relief.

It had been almost two hours when the large double doors leading to the emergency rooms slowly and magically opened. There was Josh, in a wheelchair, his thin hands clasped on his lap, his face washed-out and looking tired.

"Now you can be a nurse," Leah said, her eyes bright despite the hour.

Jayla laughed.

The next night after the kids had gone to bed, Ester was taking out the garbage when she saw Jayla at the dumpsters. There were two large dumpsters partially hidden by a grove of tall pines and spruces.

"Thank you, Ester," Jayla said, "for taking us to the hospital."

"It's what neighbors do."

"Not all neighbors."

Ester smiled. "How's Josh?"

"He's better. I'm going to try that trick of yours, with the tennis ball."

"You never know what will work."

"And that Leah—she is something," Jayla said, nodding her head. "She knows what she wants to do in life. And she's so young!"

"They've had advantages. Opportunities that a lot of people will never have." Ester remembered the trip to Florence. She would rise before everyone and get a strong coffee and sit in the empty dining room that looked over the city's clay roofs, roofs stacked like orange cards. They'd leisurely walk around the city, wide-eyed, eating whenever and whatever they wanted. The year before it was Hawaii, and that's where Leah had fallen in love with birds.

"I was thinking, Ester. You said you write grants?"

"I do."

"Maybe we could do a trade: you could help me with loans, or grants, and I could watch your kids? Take them to the park?"

"Sure."

"I'm good at taking care of people, and I always wanted to be a nurse. It's not too late. Is it? It's possible, isn't it?"

"It's always possible," Ester said, "whatever you want to do, if you want to do it badly enough."

Walking back to their apartments, the *who-whoooo* from an owl stopped them, and they both looked above and into the tall spruces, wondering what else lived there.

Rebecca Bernard

KING WHEY

My daughter Angeline sends me a picture of a tiny castle somebody left at the foot of an oak tree. It's small, would fit in the palm of your hand, and it's got these little pink and green turrets. There's a QR code sticking to the drawbridge, so I text back, *Ange, get ready to enter the dairy kingdom*, only what I mean to say, of course, is fairy kingdom, but I'm typing and walking, and I got big thumbs, so that's what I get. She's twelve, so I see three dots for a while before finally the duh emoji, the eyeroll, and I know I ruined this moment.

This moment between me and Ange who is just lately getting to the age where I no longer exist. Where she doesn't have a father because dads are lame, and way embarrassing. And when they live a state away, well, I guess they're extra easy to forget. Good riddance. Only that's not Ange, she wouldn't say that. That's the ex-wife, Cheryl. Someone who would never be invited to the dairy kingdom, not on my watch. Not if I were King of Curds.

I text her back, *hey, Ange, you know what I meant, but tell me, you on a scavenger hunt or something? you need anything, you okay?* and I see the dots again, but they never become anything. They just stay like that, wisps of a cloud, then nothing. I kiss the tips of my fingers like poof, it's gone, she's gone, the whole day up in smoke, but I know that's crazy. She's my little girl, not some butter princess going to melt away when I'm not looking.

This all gets me distracted and when I check the time, I'm late for my shift at the firehouse. No time to wonder about Ange or castles or Cheryl's new live-in asshole, Rick, or milkmaids or monsters or anything else I left behind.

Later though, when I'm at the firehouse sitting around on the big sofa we got, watching TV with a couple of the other guys, waiting for something terrible to happen because that's my life, I start thinking, what *would* a dairy kingdom look like?

There'd be milk, sure, rivers of it, maybe streams of whole or two percent, and they'd all feed together into this ocean, this great white ocean of cream. There'd be lakes, too, dark with chocolate milk, or maybe pink and creamy like strawberry, what used to be Ange's favorite when she was little-little, because hey, who's making the rules here, just me. The Gouda King William, me.

Thinking about all this gets me down, like how Ange used to like sweet things and now she probably drinks what her mom drinks, skim or not even milk at all, some oat or almond something, nothing you could call dairy. Which doesn't make sense why I care, but it's what I feel, so I try and ignore it which I used to be good at but lately—

Around five, I take our dalmatian Hatch out back to relieve himself, and because all this sitting around just gets me lonely, lets the thoughts come of what I'm missing, and it's no good, not worth it to wonder. I left town and Ange eight months back because I couldn't afford to live in the city anymore, and I'd got this lead on the fire gig and I thought to myself, okay, I can be Hero Dad, Vacation Dad, Phone Call Dad, but then as I'm packed, about to head out in the U-Haul, there's Ange staring at me like *you're leaving me with* her, *and worse yet* him, *that Rick, that goatee guy I don't even know?* And I saw she didn't get the logic of it, that she was a kid, and she didn't know money, she didn't know rent, she just knew dad was leaving, was bad, had gone bad like old milk. Spoiled. I'd spoiled the family, not getting my shit together, and now that I had, now that it was together, it was too late.

In the dairy kingdom, the clouds would be sour cream and sometimes they'd get too thick and a little would drip down and you could catch it in your mouth. Other times it'd snow and that'd be parmesan. The town dump that's limburger, of course, and then the rich part of town, there's your triple creams, your extra sharp cheddar, and none of that dyed orange stuff, the real deal, the crystally white kind from the seaside that's sharp enough to make your mouth pucker. And all the dairy dads would have good jobs, keeping the temperature cool and being steady, waking up when they're supposed to and not staying out late, and the moms and the kids would understand them even if they messed up. And all anyone would have to do to celebrate is get a cracker and break off a little piece of the world to fill them up, to make everyone feel complete, like they always got what they needed, all that calcium and vitamin D and love.

Hatch finishes up and I check my phone, and still nothing. Not even three dots. I feel ticked even though I shouldn't feel ticked, I'm working on that. But I worry, I can't help it.

I know Ange doesn't like Rick, and I don't like him either. The other day she texted me, *dad, I miss you and I wish he weren't here, I don't like the way he*—and then it was those dots again, and then nothing, and I wanted to call her, I did. But I didn't call, because? I was here. I was waiting for something bad to happen, and I didn't want to be a pain, that's right. So, I texted, *what? what Ange?* And nothing, that radio silence and then later, when I texted again, the next day or maybe the day after, she said it was nothing. It was nothing, so leave her alone.

Only how do I do that? Or maybe, how did I do that? Leave?

The house alarm rings and I'm still out front with Hatch, so I bring him inside, shoo him upstairs, then I'm jumping into my bunker gear and my boots. The bells ring and me and the other guys are on the truck, on the move.

It's just now sunset and the sky's the color of rind, all bright orangey red. We're barreling down the street, sirens blazing sharp sound, and then here's the house.

The house on fire.

The burning smells sweet, acrid, earthy. I can see the smoke billowing in the air like clouds. I'm off the truck, plugging in the hose, rushing forward on the front lawn. The second story's burning, so I raise the hose and the water arcs thick and golden in the magic hour light.

But then I see it's not water, it's buttermilk, dense and rich, and there's a little girl inside, I can see her, trapped up there in the top turret and I'm saving her, I'm going to save her, this princess of margarine, my daughter of cream.

I'm here, I shout, and the hose sprays but she's so far away, she can't hear me.

She won't hear me. The ladder pressing against the wall, crumbling, melting.

Angeline, I scream it this time. But I know there's no way.

I watch it all sour.

I let it all come burning down.

Marguerite Alley

ALL OF OUR ECCENTRIC DIVERSIONS

The package on Diana's porch contained a book, and it arrived on the Wednesday after she announced enthusiastically on Facebook her intention to climb Everest later in the spring. Returning from a jog, Diana lingered on the stoop as she cracked open the battered paperback. Inscribed in ballpoint pen on the title page were the words: *You're a fucking idiot! Love, Wendell Willkie.*

This was February in Georgia, a capricious month. The air was temperate and moist, weighted with the potential of a turn back towards winter. On the horizon was a squall line of turgid cloud, and she admired the melodrama of it as she sat down on the front step of her sagging porch. And she admired Wendell Willkie's melodrama, too. The book was Jon Krakauer's *Into Thin Air*—the account of a string of deaths on Everest in 1996.

Beneath tangerine bike shorts, her legs extended thick and white. She crossed them at the ankle and admired the flex of her calf. She was strong; she knew this, and now it was necessary to prove this fact to others. Wendell Willkie was not gloomy by nature but since their breakup and the mildly bitter attempt at friendship that followed, she sensed a certain inevitable hostility flowing back and forth between them, volleyed like a tennis ball into one another's court whenever the opportunity arose. They were making a game of misery, a team sport that required the cooperation of the other for maximum effect. He would, of course, feel compelled to tell her that Everest was a foolish endeavor. She would have done the same to him and would have expected the petty phone call to retort—an action which she now performed herself.

"I'm not going to die extravagantly on Everest," she greeted him, when he picked up on the first ring.

"Extravagance is not my concern," he said. "The idea of your totally unremarkable death on Everest is stupider than your exciting one."

"People don't die on Everest unless they do dumb shit," Diana said. "I have been well-instructed on how not to do dumb shit by the guiding company. I don't need your condescending concern."

"Wow, aren't you the expert," he said flatly, and through the phone she heard the sound of creaking wood, of cotton t-shirt sliding past chenille couch cushion. It was nearly six in the evening; he would be waking

　　　　　　　　　　　　　　　　　　　　The Louisville Review

from his habitual afternoon nap, rising from the sofa he had appropriated from the side of the road to furnish his new apartment. This was after she kicked him out of the bungalow that had been their home for two years but, notably, had been her home for longer. He said, "I had no idea you were such a prodigious mountaineer. Zero mountains climbed and you already know with such certainty what's dangerous and what's not."

"I know you think you're being clever right now but you're just being a dick." She slipped inside, kicking the door shut behind her with a bold twitch of her bad leg. Outside, the clouds crowding the sky cast the house in glaucous shades; she moved through it thickly, as though underwater, picking things up and putting them down, the phone pressed to her ear.

Wendell Willkie was silent a moment, then said snippily, "I don't think I'm being clever."

The conversation was on the precipice of a turn that she knew would be both nasty and boring. Diana switched topics but found quickly that they had little else to talk about. By the time she hung up, the rain had begun.

Wendell Willkie Scherer did not go by Wendell or Will or WW, any of which, Diana thought, would have been at least marginally less of a mouthful. He was six and a half feet tall, charmingly plump around the waist, and wore a scruffy black beard to match the length of the flow that sprung from his head and hung over his shirt collar. Occasionally, his hair grew long enough to spook him by darkly invading his peripheral vision; more than once she had seen him startle when he turned his head too quickly. He had a vaguely sentimental reason for staunchly refusing to go by anything but his two first names—which had something to do with his father, who in turn had been named for the 1940 presidential candidate—but Diana suspected that he really just insisted upon it in order to maintain a certain plateau of quirkiness. He had large, sunburned hands and little interest in traditional work, which facilitated his frequent naps and tendency to spend long hours in the backyard using a Dutch oven to boil corned beef.

Once, he had solemnly admitted that he didn't think he was cut out for a career—his professional lethargy was not a mid-twenties phase but an inherent fact of his being. It was hard to dispute this. In their relationship it was Diana who paid the mortgage and the car lease and let him borrow her card to grocery shop. Even, or perhaps especially, during the year she had been nearly bed bound. She was a software engineer,

and had worked from home eighty hours a week after the car accident
that left one of her legs broken in three places, uselessly contorted by
casts and machinery and healing surgical scars. Now, after operations
and physical therapy and patience, she was back on her feet. She was
running, standing in the kitchen, bending over fledgling tomato plants
in the garden. And she would be climbing Everest, the natural progres-
sion of her voracious work ethic. Obviously, Wendell Willkie would not
understand such a thing.

Standing at the kitchen counter post-run, she sliced cheese off a
block and paired it with a Triscuit, filling the dry, salty corners of her
mouth. She never used to be a jogger; the vicissitudes of hydration were
still a mystery to her. She felt too slow on the back half of the first mile,
and faint when she tried to sprint the last four hundred yards to her
driveway at the end of her three-mile neighborhood loop. The cat me-
andered in from the living room, matted with sleep, and came to lay at
her feet. He rolled onto his back, presented his velvet underbelly. It was
a trap, she knew—she would reach down to pet him, and he would curl
into her hand, claws out, teeth crunching down like snow under boots.

Diana was climbing Everest because Angie did, last year. Or tried to—
she was turned around by incoming bad weather only a few hundred
meters from the summit. Now she was saving up for another go at the
peak and getting a discount because she recommended Diana to Mountain Mania. For months, the guiding company had sent Diana weekly
emails containing packing lists, workouts, diets, and tips for preparing
for the harsh world ahead of her. They even offered a trip-booking service, so she didn't have to purchase her own airline ticket from Atlanta to
Kathmandu, via New York and Doha. They promised that prior climbing experience was unnecessary, that clients should not be intimidated
by talk of crampons and ice axes and snow blindness, that all would be
illuminated once they assembled in Kathmandu and began the hike up
to base camp at 17,000 feet. Having overcome a degree of ingrained
money anxiety from her approximately middle-class upbringing to com-
mit to the eighty-thousand-dollar trip, funding it mostly via cashing in
the RSUs her company gave out in lieu of bonuses, Diana was pleased
by these reassurances. There was the sense that, far off, things were being taken care of. Logistics aside, the physicality of the experience could
be focused on: she would be able to dive headfirst into the intensity of

a body finding its method of motion again, fighting its way back from stagnancy. She did not believe in half-measures; the deep end beckoned. It was the same urge that spurred her career in engineering—still feeling uncommitted to her chosen major as a sophomore in college, she'd walked into a required high-level math class, saw that she was the only girl, and decided on the spot that she would persist.

On Wednesday afternoons in the last few weeks leading up to their departure for Nepal, Angie met her in the southeast stairwell of their office complex with two old backpacks, both filled with bricks. By the third floor, Diana was usually wheezing. Angie, indomitable, had to shout at her from the flight above to *keep moving, there's a storm coming up the valley, you're in the Death Zone, the summit is just a few meters away!* A few rounds up and down the stairs and Diana was red-faced, lightheaded, prickly and liquid beneath her skin. It was pleasing, in such moments, to imagine the cold of Everest—the chill of a high altitude wind, a world of seething white, the sky a gunmetal gray. Angie said that more than once her eyes had watered so much in the breeze that the tears had frozen her eyelids together. And that the head guide, Henry, had had to press his mouth against her sealed eye until his hot breath melted the ice.

"Henry is something else," Angie said, as they perched on the bottom step and slugged water from matching turquoise Nalgenes. "I feel like in another life he was like a great war commander or something. I'd definitely follow him into battle."

Diana nodded at this, the cold seeping into her bottom from the cool concrete of the step. It was not hard to summon an image of Henry to the fore of her mind; his handsome, crunchy, rugged visage was featured heavily in Mountain Mania's promotional literature. A white man with a few days' worth of salt-and-pepper stubble, a sunburnt nose, wrap around sunglasses. And Angie had taken a plethora of pictures on last year's attempt—in one, Henry smiled roguishly up at her as he secured her crampons to her boots. The position of servitude he had contorted himself into had its own sort of appeal.

After their Wednesday work out, drinks were usually required. A Chili's around the corner from their office park did the trick, the sweat drying on their skin as they leaned over the broad, dark wood of the bar and slurped on watery cocktails, vibrant and slimy with condensation. She had met Angie because they were both verification engineers, working together to maintain and augment a debugging tool that the CPU team used for testing purposes. They had a perfunctory percentage of their preferences and beliefs in common. Most of the time, Diana felt such a rush of relief to see another woman around the office that she gave hardly any thought to whether she genuinely liked Angie. Even as she found Angie's intensity both admirable and off-putting. Even when she looked across a conference table as some particularly pompous man expounded on the obvious, hoping to catch Angie's eye and exchange words in that silent, innate language, only to find the other woman looking anywhere but at her. Angie had a cultivated impenetrability, an athlete's blank potency. A person who did hard things because they were hard, and because others did not. She had been a pentathlete in college, and this was not hard to imagine—her long, lithe legs arcing over hurdles, her hearty, freckled shoulders tossing a shot put. Her hair was flaxen and straight as reeds and visibly dry at the ends when she turned her head quickly, her ponytail fanning against Diana's cheek. The fact that someone like Angie was climbing Everest was so unsurprising that it required no justification; coworkers acknowledged this fact with one raised eyebrow, perhaps two on a boring Tuesday afternoon, and no further questions.

"God, it's such a rush," Angie mused, tearing a damp napkin to shreds with quick little flicks of the square French tip on her pointer finger. "I can't fucking wait to get up there again. That's *living*. You think you're living now, but you're not. Trust me."

Diana often looked for some trace of irony or humor when Angie spoke like this but had yet to find any. "I talked to Wendell Willkie yesterday," Diana said. "Naturally he thinks I don't know what I'm getting myself into."

Angie rolled her eyes. "And what would he know?"

In the month since their break-up, Diana had found it difficult not to bring up Wendell Willkie in at least every other conversation she had. There was a certain humor to his mere existence that she took pleasure in entertaining her friends with. When he was twenty-one, he had spent six months at a nudist commune; at twenty-three he'd walked across the state of Tennessee with a shopping cart on a bet. In her life, he had been reduced to a collection of amusing stories, made all the more amusing by the idea of his dating Diana, who was by all accounts a sensible woman. The kind with a job and a modest mortgage and a lack of mental health issues. Before she bought her Toyota Camry (secondhand, silver, gray cotton upholstery) she had made spreadsheets to weigh the pros and cons of similarly priced midsize sedans. And she had been through a lot recently, as she was often tactfully reminded of by concerned friends as her leg healed. She was aware that this collection of facts made the Everest idea palatable.

Diana was a rational girl, despite her somewhat baffling taste in whimsical men, so therefore summiting Everest must be a rational proposition. This was what she had reasoned through when the idea first occurred to her, a year ago when the end of her convalescence was in sight, and she was watching Angie's trip photos wash through her Instagram feed. There was cell reception at base camp, which made such transmissions easy—she felt almost as if she was sharing the experience alongside the other woman, huffing across crevasses and up the faces of glaciers and along sparkling icy ridges with clear eyes and pumping, flexing quadriceps. But the need to see for herself had grown from a passing thought into an obsession and had begun, perhaps subconsciously, to motivate her as she trawled through the last phase of her physical therapy. Then she was on her feet again, Angie was back in the country, and the only barrier to her own entry into the same high-altitude, high-octane world was a check drawn from her savings account and mailed to Mountain Mania.

After the drink with Angie, Diana pondered how to spend her evening. Post-recovery, she often had this feeling: that there were too many options available to her at any given moment to reasonably respond to. She could break into a sprint, if she wished. She could go cliff diving or wander between the aisles of a grocery store, ad infinitum. The bad thing had happened, it had reached her, she had endured it—now all that remained was the smooth ribbon of the future, wherein she could move unimpeded, a vessel equipped and maintained for perpetual motion. Sitting in the front seat of her car, she consulted her phone for options. Due to her search history, articles were recommended to her with titles like "Inside the Bottleneck: Everest's Deadliest Season" and "Tricks and Tips for Pacing Yourself on Summit Day" and "Green Boots: The Body of a Climber That Has Become a Landmark on the Route to the Top." Mountain Mania's weekly email had come in as well, detailing an amped up workout regimen as the departure date neared. Henry Meyers was quoted in the last paragraph, espousing his views on the level of motivation that one needed to make it to the top. *You can't allow anything to stop you, he wrote. No matter how tired you feel, no matter who around you gives up, you've got to be single-minded about your desire to reach the end. That being said, safety first.*

She decided that it would be back to the house for dinner preparation, which was usually when she felt Wendell Willkie's absence most
keenly. A hybrid of nostalgia and bitterness, lingering like the clotted
residue of a barcode sticker, stood beside her as she rinsed kale in the
sink. Wendell Willkie was uncontested in the culinary arts, when he
could be bothered to employ them. A Reuben he'd made for her two
years ago was still in her top ten sandwiches of all time. With her credit
card he'd bought a toaster that could be set to only darken bread on one
side, and then applied a slick of Russian dressing to the slabs of marbled
pumpernickel-and-rye he laid carefully before him on the kitchen island. Then sauerkraut, warm and soft and shot through with vinegar,
and a creamy tide of swiss cheese, and finally a collection of corned beef
shavings, pink and fatty and tender. He had always had strong opinions
about the quality of the meat they needed to buy, regardless of the state
of her credit card balance. The Reuben process was almost alchemical,
so precise and teleological that she wasn't sure she had wanted to witness it—as if consuming the details of a thing, the creation of it, dimin-
ished its capacity for beauty. The sandwiches ready, Wendell Willkie had
popped open a bottle of wine and waved it around in the air for a few
moments. "You have to let it breathe," he said.

"Why?" she asked.

"I don't know," he said, and shrugged. "It's just something people
say."

She was training for Everest, now, regaining the physical fitness sto-
len from her due to her long recuperation and Wendell Willkie's dietary
opulence. There was no room for bread, rye or otherwise, in her caloric
intake. This was a question entirely of athleticism, rather than of shape.
She and Wendell Willkie had been happy and pear-shaped for most of
their time together. She had always had an unusual degree of indifference
about the state of her figure, and now such apathy felt justified—she was
healthy again, her joints moving in easy tandem, the pain fully receded
into whatever knotty crevices had produced it, so what else mattered?
This speech to friends and family always set a few heads bobbing ear-
nestly, the women cooing their agreement and not believing a word of
it. What did matter, she had told herself, was the next hurdle, the run
up the south slope of Everest, and nothing else. She looked around the
empty room and consoled herself with this vision of triumph.

But the house did feel indisputably quiet these days. The yard was
getting scrubby, darkening the windows with shiny kudzu. She still

found orphaned socks of his, faded with age and washing, mixed in with her laundry. Wendell Willkie, even separate of his looming height, had been a large presence—from her bed she would hear him humming as he cooked, or the brisk scraping sound of his welding torch in the garage as he concocted something tangentially useful out of scrap metal harvested from abandoned cars. Now, she felt as though another presence moved in the house, living a shadow life beneath hers, waiting for her to turn on the rattling tap or close a squeaking door so that it could make noise of its own. She wondered if she should sell the place and move, if the specter of her injury and Wendell Willkie's attentive caretaking in its aftermath were too much of a combination to endure in her new life of adventure and extremity. In her mind, this house would always be one in which she was helpless, prostrate, laid bare by the shock of pain that used to travel through her like a gale whenever she moved her healing limbs. There were rooms that held time like a cup holds water, where you could drown in the accumulation of layered years—where you could get a foot snagged under a rock, lay stagnant in the current, start growing moss.

Wendell Willkie called again as she was tossing the kale in a lemony dressing, sprinkling in pine nuts with her left hand. When she picked up, he said, "I think you have a masochistic tendency."

She snorted. "That's very pop psychology of you."

"How are you?" he asked. "Your leg holding up okay?"

A streak of defensiveness flared in her, then subsided. "No problems at all."

"I've been reading about Everest," he said. "About the environmental concerns. And the exploitations of the Sherpas."

"Looking to join us?" she asked, smiling sardonically into the kale at the thought. "Did you know only, like, 10% of climbers are women?"

"Is that a real statistic or did you just make that up?"

"I don't know," she said. "Sounds real."

"I'm not sure this is the best method of affirming your feminist agenda."

"It's not an agenda," she said, and then glanced at the window above the sink. Her reflection off the black of the night startled her; she saw herself in fragments, her angles lit sporadically by the yellow overhead light. "It's just my life."

"And you're putting it in danger." This was a phrase that she thought should have been imbued with the requisite drama of love and concern, a kind of fear wrapped in vaguely erotic passion, but out of Wendell

Willkie's mouth it sounded only tired.

"You're busting my balls here," she said, affecting a caricatured New York accent, and was comforted when his laugh crackled into her ear.

During the year she spent in bed, they had gone through a number of routines to manage the time when she was not draped over her laptop trying to work. She wanted to do at least some portion of the chores; Wendell Willkie obligingly brought her baskets of laundry to fold, then placed them in the appropriate drawers once she was finished. He taught her how to play cribbage, and they kept a running game going on the bedside table, the pegs moving around the board in infinite rotations, the maintenance of a lead more important than any hypothetical win. And, in the evenings, they worked their way through a list of the best movies of all time, an astounding number of which turned out to be gangster movies set in New York City and starring, almost without exception, a collection of similar-looking white men. The accent, with all its rough-cut phrases and wide-open vowels, had begun to creep its way into their speech; when they realized what was happening, they exaggerated it to comic effect. "Fuggedaboutit" became a frequent refrain between them, both unclear on what exactly it was supposed to mean. Wendell Willkie had never been to New York at all; she'd been once as a child. Now, she thought fondly of the city, saw it in her mind's eye as eternally in the sepia-toned seventies of the movies, populated by compact men with slick hair and watchful eyes. Men who were the opposite of Wendell Willkie. Men who dealt only in violence, who expressed love through pain, through dominance, through survival.

Moving out had required Wendell Willkie to leave behind a number of items that he had decided were not worth shoving into the hatchback. One of them was a print of a colonial-era map of the Delmarva Peninsula, so criss-crossed with rivers and estuaries that it looked like a gnarled and rotten turnip, or a withered chicken's foot. Hanging as it did on the wall across from her side of the bed they once shared, it was often the first thing her eyes focused on in the morning. For months it had been such a part of her daily landscape that she felt that the image of it existed somewhere deep within her retina, that it would burn brightly in the decaying, gelatinous mold of her eye long after she was dead. It would coexist beside the one coherent image she possessed of the accident that had nearly taken her life and limbs—wherein she watched her windshield fill with the panorama of a cloudless sky, in the second before the glass shattered into unknown thousands of white lightning bolts. The car had been airborne. She had been spirited upwards, however briefly, after the eighteen-wheeler had propelled her over the jersey barrier. When she came down, life was a blur of color and fear. There were sights and sounds she still couldn't make sense of—time spent in the crumpled remains of the car, her careful extrication, the removal to the ambulance. And then, finally, the first image that she understood: Wendell Willkie appearing in the hospital, arriving at her bedside and taking her hand in his two much larger ones. He might have said something. *It's going to be okay*, perhaps. But all she knew was that he was there, his hands were warm, the breadth of his shoulders was a comfort. He had come for her.

They had been together only a few months at that point, but within two weeks after the accident Wendell Willkie had moved into her house and was directing the modification of her bed so that she could recover from home. Her leg, when not invaded by a sourceless ache, was stiff and useless—she had months of physical therapy ahead of her as they patched the bone and muscle back together. Wendell Willkie, without fanfare, stepped easily into the role of caretaker. If not interested in a career, he was no stranger to work; in fact, he excelled in the doing of things, in all the little household necessities that Diana, even when well, felt too overwhelmed by her job to properly see to. What Wendell Willkie really wasn't cut out for was money, or the structures around it—its exchange and accumulation and management. He was compelled to do useful things as they occurred to him, as they affected his immediate life or hers, and seemed indifferent to the thought that someone might pay him to do such things in another setting. He was inscrutable in this way; she could detect nothing in him of her own keen interest in the usual wax and wane of personal finance via vigorous employment. She searched for evidence of some innate economic privilege present in his background—a trust fund or some other dubious source of imminent inheritance—but found only the same unremarkable middle-class childhood that she herself had had. Whatever economic detachment Wendell Willkie had fostered internally, he seemed to have grown it himself. Something that came from nothing; the truest of miracles.

And after a year, Diana was walking again, her gait changed but steady. She was able to look around her life again and found that, in her absence, Wendell Willkie had expanded to fill her entire world. By saving her he had supplanted her, somehow. In her own house she was playing second fiddle; being ensconced in his plush arms was suddenly stifling. It was unfair, perhaps, to try to excise him so completely, after all that he had done to keep her afloat, and that was perhaps why she still answered his phone calls and made attempts to maintain a form of passive aggressive friendship with him. But once she had found all of his things—welding gloves and loose screws and coverless books on bird-watching—spread with such casual entitlement around her living room, her backyard, populating the backseat of her Toyota, there only seemed one way out.

Once, at night in that bed in which she had all but melded with the sheets, Wendell Willkie confessed that he sometimes wondered if he was a bad person. Diana thought of all the selfless acts he performed for her each day to keep her from dissolving, with only the vaguest return ever expected. He thought he might be bad. If that was true, she thought, then god help whatever she was.

Angie often described Everest in military terms, in the vocabulary of war. It was an epic battle against nature, one that required a devotion to a just cause, she said. And it took no prisoners. This appealed to something visceral and unarticulated in Diana—the sense that she wanted a good fight, the kind where the enemy is vanquished and we're all home by Christmas. She wanted to be vindicated by a clean victory, a thing she thought might have existed somewhere in the distant past but now could only be found on a peak where everything extraneous had to be stripped away. Where pain was finite and active, dealt with on one's feet rather than lying on one's back. Where matters were of life and death importance but there was a choice in it; one had to choose to live. There was no one coming to the rescue. She thought of all the stories of incapacitated climbers left to die on the slopes because their comrades would have died too if they tried to carry them down and knew that she should be repulsed by the mere idea of ever being presented with such an ethical dilemma. Knew this and, all the same, felt her chest tighten with something that was not quite fear, but perhaps a little like it.

Five days before their flight to Kathmandu was scheduled to leave, Angie came over to help her begin the packing process. Mountain Mania had provided a list, which Diana printed for easy consultation and to which Angie added items with a few flicks of a ballpoint pen. The cat, sensing an imminent departure, settled into the empty duffel bag she had unzipped on the floor. On the bed, Diana laid out stacks of long underwear, wool pullovers, a down jacket in sleek navy blue. She packed her new boots, selected from Dick's Sporting Goods—a pair of La Sportivas that set her back a few hundred dollars, emblazoned with a fluorescent yellow stripe up the side, and that would hopefully not turn her heels to ground beef. Angie had stories of insoles soaked with blood, feet worn down to the bone. They consulted on the number of pairs of socks required, then added a few for contingency's sake. Clif bars were stashed in inner pockets for quick energy, if needed, and Diana took a moment to appreciate the drama of such a hypothetical moment. She saw herself, hunched against the wind, devouring food like a ravenous, self-aware gremlin, pared down to an awareness of only the essential functions of the body and grinning into the flying snow. When she shared this image with Angie, the reply came without a hint of irony: "That's freedom, baby."

Leisure goods were decided upon next. Diana insisted on the inclusion of an e-reader, though Angie assured her that she'd be too tired to read. Diana picked up the copy of *Into Thin Air* from the side table and said, "Is it taboo to bring this, do you think?"

Angie barked out a laugh. "I can't believe Wendell gave that to you. That's so fucked."

"I haven't had time to read it," Diana said.

"Me neither," said Angie. "But apparently it's pretty grim. A lot of people died that year."

"Did anyone die last year?"

Angie shrugged. "Nobody I knew that well. But I saw a few guys who looked like they were in rough shape."

"What do you mean?"

"I think some guy had a stroke?" Angie paused, a slim finger pressed to her chin in thought. "I remember seeing, like, three Sherpas trying to get someone down because no one else could help. I was still on my way up to the summit at that point so—" She trailed off, then shrugged again, a helpless smile pulling on her mouth.

"So, you didn't stop to see what happened to him."

"No, I couldn't," Angie said. "You'll see when you're up there. If you stop moving you never start again. You don't want to end up like me—paying all the fees a second time and tromping back up there for another go."

She punctuated this with a laugh, leaning back against the wall. Angie had expressed these sentiments before. There was only one way to do this, she said, and that was to invest entirely in one's own abilities. On the mountain, there was no ethical choice. The choice had already been made, she said, and the only way was up.

In the few remaining days before departure, Diana indulged in comforts she knew would not be forthcoming for some time: a hot bath, a trip through the Bojangles drive-thru, a nap on her lush couch. She woke up feeling disoriented, confused by the changed light as the day faded away into concentrations of shadows. The regular flow of time appeared to have receded with the sun, and when she looked out the back door into the yard it seemed that all the flora had retreated back into winter again, that this brief peek at spring had been an illusion. The still air, when she trotted out to take the trash cans to the curb, smelled the way a flat sea looks.

In the evening, Wendell Willkie texted her about whether he'd left a pair of flip flops in the hall closet. She found them tucked beneath a bulk quantity of toilet paper and sent him a picture to confirm they were the right ones. He asked if he could come on Saturday to retrieve them. This was the day she was to begin her journey to Nepal, but the first leg of the many flights ahead of her didn't depart until late afternoon. When she told him that he could come in the morning, he responded with enough enthusiasm to merit an exclamation point—*OK, great, thanks!*—and this, for some reason, made her feel unequivocally terrible for the rest of the night.

On Saturday, Wendell Willkie appeared on her porch wearing shorts cut off above the knee and a threadbare Father John Misty shirt. It was an ensemble that left her almost taken aback, wondering if he had always dressed with such hipster disdain or if this was his method of post-break-up reinvention. Both options disturbed her. He was late, and she was already waiting on Angie to arrive so they could carpool to the airport. Under his left arm, he carried a full head of cabbage.

"Some guy gave me a free cabbage on the way here," was all the explanation he gave as she let him in the screen door. "I'm gonna boil the fuck out of it when I get home, make Irish stew or something."

"I've been meaning to ask you for your lemon bar recipe," she said. "I want to make something for my coworkers when I get back."

"Trying to guilt them into asking about your trip?" he asked, with a twitch upwards of his eyebrows that she still thought was sort of charming, even when wreathed in smug superiority.

"Why else?" she quipped, and felt proud for doing so in the heat of the moment. She had been fidgety all morning, flitting around as she packed and repacked bags. She had never thought of herself as a nervous flyer, but this would be her first post-accident flight. She would be trotting through airports on rebuilt bones, squeezing into economy seats with a leg molded anew.

Wendell Willkie's eyes fell on the suitcases piled by the door. "Feeling ready?"

"Yep."

"No nerves?"

"None." She was irritated, now; his incredulity was patronizing, a general caretaking trend turned paternalist. She nodded toward his flip flops, placed next to the door, and hoped he would take the hint.

"You're not taking this seriously if you're not nervous," he said.

"And what would you know about it?" she said, and before he could reply: "Please, tell me what credential you have to give me advice about this."

She expected him to answer her with the same force as she had posed the question to him. That old urge to fight, to struggle, was pushing itself into her mouth. For so long, he had been the target of that urge; she would get a few last jabs in before she directed that energy toward the summit. Instead, he was quiet for a long while, inspecting the cabbage wedged beneath his arm. When he spoked, it was with a voice as thin as an autumn leaf. "I just want you to be safe."

"I am safe," she said.

He was still looking downwards, but she could see in the set of his mouth that he was upset. More upset than she'd realized. And had been for a while—she could see it, now that she was looking at him as a person standing in what was once their living room, rather than just a voice on the phone.

"Will you let someone take care of you if you get hurt?" he asked.

All those months in bed, fed and clothed and cleaned by his hands alone. Did he really love her to such a degree of selfless annexation? Or was that just his nature? Neither were truths she felt able to understand.

She thought of Angie's words, of all of her diatribes about self-reliance on the mountain. The dead and dying left behind when they collapsed into the snow, the choice already made by everyone else to continue no matter what. This was the world ahead of her, a world that had always existed outside of the two of them in this house. A ringing in her ears began, a sound like a far-off whistle, traveling steadily toward her. Dread like an arriving train.

"I'm not going to get hurt," she said.

"Can I hug you?"

In his embrace, she inhaled the smell of him. Warm garden dirt, the citrus tang of Gojo pumice soap, baked-in sweat in the fraying collar of his shirt. The length of his arms felt as though they could have encircled her twice. "I'm really going to be fine," she said, into his neck. She steadied herself against his body, the expanse of him a necessary structural support. "Anybody can climb Everest these days. It's really no big deal."

Tenderly, he said, "You're fucking delusional, Di."

When he pulled away she entertained, however briefly, the idea of inviting him to come with her. At least to Kathmandu. A last minute ticket, surely, could be obtained. He could hold her hand on the flight, see her off when the guiding company led her into the Himalayan foothills. He could be there for her, as he had been in the hospital, warm hands at the ready.

The thought disappeared from her mind as quickly as it had appeared. Angie was pulling into the driveway, leaning on the horn. It occurred to her, abruptly, that she had never asked Angie why it was she had wanted to climb Everest in the first place. Somehow it had never come up and Angie, who had always held herself to a high degree of aloofness, had never volunteered her motive, if there was one at all.

Wendell Willkie glanced outside, then back at Diana. She felt her hands begin to tremble, the way they used to at the end of a long PT session. He seemed unsurprised to be finding her, once again, as vulnerable as a human could be before him. She looked at him, eyes wide.

"I'm sure you'll be alright," he said, finally.

She knew, then, that if he asked her to stay at that moment, she would have done it. He did not ask. He carried her bags outside, walked her to the passenger side of Angie's car, and waved her off into whatever was to come next.

S. A. Griffin

The Wrong Door

The first time I went to the poet's apartment, I mistook his closet door for the front door when I was trying to leave. The poet told me that mistake was common since the two doors are close to each other, and that some people, in a rush, had even stepped into the closet before they realized their mistake. For me, it wasn't haste that led me to open the closet door, but confusion. In fact, I was not eager to leave at all.

I came to know the poet when we worked together as proofreaders for a textbook company. I was then, as I am now, a struggling painter. It was a poorly run company. The poet and I were made to share a desk in a back room with bad lighting. An air vent directly over our desk blew my hair in my face if I didn't fasten it back in a barrette. We were paid very little. Also, the textbooks were terrible. The information was so oversimplified that it wasn't true. When we brought this up with our boss, he reminded us these were books for middle school, as if that were a sufficient answer. It was demoralizing to work in a place like that even if it was just a way to pay our bills and not our vocation.

The poet would often be late, and when he got to the office he'd say the reason was because he hadn't been able to figure out which shoes to wear, or what clothes to put on. It wasn't that he was a fussy dresser, it was that he had difficulty making decisions. Not only that, once he made a decision it was likely wrong; he came in T-shirts when it was cold out and long-sleeved button-downs in the heat. He complained about being uncomfortable but blamed it on the office's poor ventilation. I liked to wait and see if he was going to be late and what he would be wearing when he got there. I liked it when he was late and ill-dressed. The more difficulty he had dealing with the day, the more I liked him.

One day he rushed into work late and before he'd set down his bundle of newspaper, he addressed me with great purpose. "I need your advice." It occurred to me that he was going to ask me for my help with a dating situation, and my stomach sank in preparation. By this time, we'd been working together for several weeks, and I'd noticed a growing attraction to him. I thought he might feel the same toward me though I couldn't be sure because his behavior was hard to decipher, and there was a large age difference between us, which could either be a deterrent or enticement for him. It was a twelve-year difference with me on the upper end. Most of the time I didn't feel older than him since my life circumstances were very much the same as his. But when I made the mistake of looking in the mirror under harsh lighting, I had to admit my youth was slipping away. What surprised me most about my aging face was how unattractive I was becoming.

Youth can do a lot for the not-so-pretty face. Everything is taut in youth so that even a face that lacks cheekbones and a strong jaw line can look good. Later, however, flaws will surface. Without cheekbones and a jaw line, the entire face sags straight into the thickening neck so that there is no definition between the two. You end up a neck-face, like that graffiti that's everywhere (though I doubt that the young male graffiti artist had a middle-aged female in mind when he came up with his character). I'm well on my way to becoming a neck-face, I'd say I'm about 80 percent there.

"I bought a painting I can't afford, and I don't know whether I should stop payment on my check and return it," the poet said. "I bought it directly from the artist. I wrote her a check, and I even said, 'Should I wait and pick it up after my check clears?' and she said no, she trusted me to take it now. So, it would be bad if I stopped payment on my check, wouldn't it?"

"Well, not if you can't afford it," I said.

"I don't know if I can," he said. "I can afford it now, but I might not be able to pay my next batch of bills."

He'd met the artist at a party when they'd gotten into a conversation about her work. It turned out that she lived in the building where the party was being held, and she invited the poet to her apartment to take a look at her work. He admired one painting in particular, and she told him he could have it at a discounted price. He felt it would be insulting not to buy it, and so he wrote the check and took the painting home with him in a cab, which was also more money out of his pocket he hadn't planned on spending.

"Maybe you'd want it," he said.

"You want me to buy the painting from you?" I said. "You could never have her over to your place because she would wonder where the painting is." I said this because I thought there might have been more going on between them than the painting, and I wanted to find out.

"I'm not going to have her over."

"Ever?" I said.

"You might like it," he said. "It's good actually. You can come over and look at it. I'd sell it to you for even less than I paid."

I thought it unlikely that I would want the doubly discounted painting. I had enough of my own bad work lying around. But I wanted to go to the poet's place and spend time with him outside of the demeaning job, and I wondered if he too perhaps wanted to invite me over and this offered him the excuse. I told him I would look at it.

His apartment was small, which didn't surprise me given his financial situation. It was an alcove studio apartment. The main room included a galley kitchen and was only big enough to fit his one battered couch and two overstuffed bookshelves. In the alcove was a single bed. Shirts were hung on a rod above it. The painting was leaning against a bare wall. As I predicted, I was not impressed. It was sort of Medieval-looking, technically good, but what's the point? "Not bad," I said.

The poet darted over to the refrigerator and flung it open. "Do you want anything to drink? Water? Wine? Let's have wine." He poured two glasses of chilled white wine and handed one to me. We sat on the couch with our glasses while he waited for me to say something more about the painting.

"It's nice. Why don't you take it?" he said.

"Why don't you keep it? It's not bad."

"I'll give you a good price."

"It's not that," I said. "It's just that I don't have anywhere to put it." My apartment was only slightly larger than the poet's, but the layout was worse. It was long and narrow, like a bowling alley, with one tiny window at the end.

"Let it sink in for a while. Don't decide yet," he said. "Maybe it'll grow on you."

He leapt up from the couch and snapped on the radio, which was tuned to a college station. He poured me more wine. He seemed nervous and glad to have me there. He didn't mention the painting again and neither did I because I was afraid that as soon as I made a decision about it, there would be no more reason to be there, and I would have to leave.

We brought up the topic of dinner, but the poet didn't have any food in his place to offer me, and we couldn't decide if we should order in or go out, and finally we decided we weren't that hungry after all. We finished the bottle of white and then the poet opened a bottle of red.

He told me he was sick of living in such poverty, having to make his meager check stretch too far. "But then what do I really want?" he said. "I don't want a front lawn with sprinklers and a garage door opener."

"I know," I said. "Who wants that? It would just be nice to be able to go into a store and buy a pair of shoes without having to calculate all the sacrifices it's going to take to afford them."

"Right," he said. "I don't care about clothes or shoes. I'll go to the Salvation Army. But what's going to happen when I get old? I can't be this poor when I'm old. If I am you'll have to shoot me." I considered it a good sign that he expected to still know me in his old age.

As the night wore on, the poet began to sit closer to me on the couch. He put his arm behind me, so that it was grazing my back, then he removed it and apologized. At one point he rested his head on my shoulder, so that his hair brushed my neck in a pleasant way, but he quickly lifted his head and said sorry. This sort of thing continued through the night, in which he would make an affectionate gesture and then apologize for it.

In between his strange, conflicting impulses, we talked about many things. We told each other stories from our childhoods, named our favorite products, and relayed snippets of overheard conversations. We talked about how we interpreted our world. He told me he'd given shapes to the days of the week and that his Monday was pleated like an accordion and Saturday was an oversized bell. I loved hearing these descriptions. Who but him has a pleated Monday? Here is a person I would never tire of, I thought to myself.

By the time we'd almost finished the second bottle of wine, it had gotten quite late, and the poet suggested that I spend the night. He said it was too late and I was too drunk to get home. But because he had only made these tentative, unclear moves toward intimacy and had not kissed me, I was uncertain what this suggestion to spend the night was supposed to mean. I couldn't tell if it was out of concern for my safety, or if there was more to it. But once I said I would stay, we both rose and went into his alcove. He had several notebooks stacked on his bed, so I had to wait while he moved them to the floor before we could get in. I couldn't prop myself up on my elbows or else the shirts hanging overhead would hit me in the face, so I lay flat.

"What do you want to do?" the poet said. "Go to sleep or not?"

I knew what he was getting at, though it was difficult to answer because he'd put it so oddly. "I'm not that tired," I said. And that seemed to be sufficient to set things in motion.

I was thankful for the darkness of the windowless alcove as we removed our clothes in the narrow bed. I would have liked to see the contours of the poet's twenty-seven-year-old body, but I didn't want my own on-the-brink-of-middle-age body on display. We were not careful and slow the way it often is with someone new; instead, we sped along, not speaking a word or making a sound. There was no lingering on unimportant body parts. It was as if the poet had been assigned a task and was eager to complete it. Very quickly a condom was retrieved, but once the unfurling began, he was no longer in operating order, and it all came to an abrupt end.

"Sorry," he said. I had never gotten an apology before in these circumstances, and I found it thoughtful and noble that he should take the responsibility. We lay close but turned away from each other. I wondered if he would make another attempt, but he remained still. Eventually we drifted off to sleep, though it was problematic in the tiny bed, and I woke up a few times with my arm dead asleep above my head so that I had to lift it with my other arm and move it by my side to get the feeling back.

In the morning, when the poet got up to use the bathroom, I gathered my clothes and quickly dressed. He came back wearing a flannel robe, sat on the edge of the bed, and started talking about what a difficult person he is and how he "always ruins everything." I said I wasn't good at relationships either. He said he didn't want to talk anymore and say wrong things. I realized I shouldn't have said the word "relationship." I told him I wished to stay and rectify the situation, but he said no and ushered me into the main room where I reluctantly said goodbye and tried to leave through the closet door. I laughed at myself and stood there grateful for the delay my mistake allowed, but then I had to use the real door and leave.

He didn't call me later that day or the next as I'd hoped. I tried to keep busy so I wouldn't notice, but everything I did was done with a sick feeling in my stomach, so it wasn't a very successful strategy. Finally, I calmed myself down with the thought that the weekend was nearly over and I would soon see him.

But he was not at the proofreading job on Monday. I asked my boss what happened to the poet, and he said he didn't know, he hadn't heard from him. My boss was unfazed, probably used to people quitting on him without notice. I left several messages for the poet over the next few days but heard nothing back.

I could no longer stand working at the small, cramped table by myself. And I couldn't stand sitting alone in my bowling alley apartment staring at my paints and doing nothing. My parents had a seldom-used summer cabin that I would sometimes escape to. So, one morning, instead of going in to work, I took the train upstate.

I thought the country would be a good break. I told myself I was going there to devote myself to painting. But as soon as I was in the country, I wanted to be back in the city. I didn't like being so far from the poet, even though I felt far from him in the city too. There were flies in the country house. I had to hang fly strips and walk from room to room with a fly swatter in my hand. Nor was it quiet in the country as I'd expected. There was construction going on nearby, and all day long I heard the sound of power tools. I couldn't settle myself anywhere. If I found a room with good light for painting, it was too noisy, if I closed the window, it became too hot. I only got as far as stretching a canvas and setting it on my easel. I never even took out my paints.

I'd been in the country for about a week, thinking of nothing but the poet and the awkward night we'd spent together and the terrible next morning, when I met another man. I met this man at the garden center where I'd gone to buy some plants that I'd decided to put in a painting I was finally thinking about. I wanted to paint a virgin straddling a fence with many lush, flowering jungle plants in the background. I thought I'd put a beekeeper's hood on the virgin.

I had started a wagon of potted plants in the greenhouse, and I was beginning to like the look of them, so many different kinds of flowers and colors and shapes bunched together, fronds bouncing as I pulled them down the aisle. My wagon of plants made me feel buoyant and pleased for the first time since I'd been in the country. This is when the man appeared. He had a wagon of his own, though he was pulling flats of dirt. He asked me about my selection, and I told him what they were for.

"You're going to paint them?" he said. "I'm going to plant mine."

"What are yours?"

"They're begonias. They will be. I'm putting in a quarter-acre flower garden and a fishpond myself. You should come and see it."

I was glad to have the attention of another man, and I accepted his invitation though I was not ready to like anyone but the poet. This man at the garden center had graying hair, wore bifocals, and looked like a father, which, it turns out, he was. He had two grown children in their twenties though he was only a little older than me. He'd been divorced for years.

His house was in the next village over from my family's house. It was up a winding dirt road and set back at the foot of the hills. There was a slate porch behind the house and a walkway leading to an open area where he was putting in the garden. Wood stakes marked where the pond was to go.

After I was shown the future garden and pond, I was brought into the house and given the "grand tour." As I might have expected, this man's house was very different from the poet's dinky apartment. There were polished hardwood floors and large windows draped in sheer fabric, held back by brass stays. It was nicely furnished with plush couches and armchairs, and both bedrooms had queen-size beds with quilts spread tightly and pillows propped expertly against the headboard. The tour ended in the kitchen where he'd laid out a plate of cheeses, crackers, fruit, and olives, and two wine glasses next to a bottle of California wine. As we ate, he narrated the snacks, giving many details about the cheeses, their origins, how they were manufactured, the curing procedure of the olives, the history of the wine. When we were finished, he took me to an organic restaurant.

He asked what I would like and when the waiter came, he placed my order. Over dinner he asked me many questions about myself, which at first, I enjoyed, but soon became a burden. I didn't want to tell him one more thing about myself, but I didn't know how to stop him, and so I went on answering his questions but became vague and evasive. He seemed to take no notice of my withdrawal and launched into a story of his own. He said he'd tried his hand at writing once. He'd decided to write a novel and so he'd spent each morning thinking about what to write and then the rest of a full eight-hour day typing out those thoughts quickly before they escaped him. He said he was a fairly good typist and still it had taken him a long time to complete the novel—three months! He said it probably wasn't very good. On the other hand, he said it wasn't awful and perhaps he'd try to "do something" with it. I imagined what the poet would think of him and his quick-typing method of writing. Can you believe this guy? I thought. No, the poet shook his head, he couldn't.

As the night continued, I realized that the poet had taken up residence in my mind and was providing commentary on the scene. My date had a habit of saying "at the end of the day," which the poet found annoying. When my date talked about his upbringing in the very village where he now owned his house and his reluctance to go to the city, the poet thought him provincial.

When dinner was finished my date said that rather than order dessert and coffee at the restaurant, he had a delicious gooseberry pie he baked himself and "real" coffee back at his place. I told him I was tired and asked him to take me home. He wanted to know if he could call me the next day. I said he could, though I wasn't at all certain I wanted to hear from him.

When he called me the next day as promised, I accepted another date with him. He continued to call to ask me out, and each time I would waver and then accept, and in this way, we began an affair.

One nice thing about spending time with the country man was how much more of the country I saw with him than I'd ever seen before. In all the years I'd spent at my family's house, I'd never ventured far. But now I was like a member of the Explorer's Club, boating some waterway, biking up tough mountains, hiking gorges, and swimming under waterfalls. But throughout these activities I felt distant from the country man; my mind was always on the poet. If I stood on the edge of the shore with my fishing pole, it was the poet who was next to me with a pole of his own. When I struggled to bike to the top of a hill, the poet rode alongside saying encouraging words. And when it came time to sit on the blanket under a tree and eat a picnic lunch, the poet turned up his lip at the high-end gourmet selections the country man had packed, and suggested we pick wild blueberries instead.

I conversed with the poet so extensively in my head that I hadn't noticed how quiet I actually was. Every so often the country man would ask me if I was okay. "You're awfully quiet," he would say. "Is something wrong?"

"Oh was I being quiet?" I'd say. "I didn't realize."

There was one moment when I had a strong feeling for the country man. It was one day when we went for a hike to a lake, and we'd worn our bathing suits under our clothes. The sun was very bright, and when I took off my clothes and saw the way my body looked in that light—my extreme paleness, the rippled flesh, the wrinkly skin—my spirit sank.

I'd never seen myself look as old and worn as I did that afternoon in my bathing suit out in the bright sun. It was obvious that I was well beyond my peak. Who would ever want me now? I thought, and then the country man smiled at me and ran his hand down my arm. This man, I thought, is who.

But in the dark of the bedroom, I didn't appreciate his desire as I had in the sunlight. At times his eagerness put me off and I'd have to let my mind wander to get over the hump and be receptive to him again. My mind often wandered to the poet.

Soon I realized that the poet had become my constant companion, there to listen to my thoughts and observations. I spent my time with the country man, but the poet was there too, and in some ways, perhaps because he always said the sharpest things, he was even more present than the country man. He took great pleasure in the things I had to say. He found me amusing and original.

I had gotten so used to the poet in this form that when I got an actual message on my machine from the real man, I had to sit down and absorb the meaning. He was calling to invite me to a reading he would be giving. It was to take place the next day. He'd ended the message with "Hope you can make it." I replayed those words in my head a number of times. I wondered what sort of thought processes he'd undergone to be able to say those words to me. I wondered if he'd gone through any of his own interior torture over what had happened and wondered what it was he hoped for now.

When the country man called me later that day, I told him I was going down to the city for a few days, and he invited himself along.

"You don't like the city," I said.

"I like anywhere you are," he said. I knew it was a nice sentiment, yet I had no appreciation for his words. I could think only of this man encroaching on my reunion with the poet, and I told him rather harshly that I had a number of things to take care of that I needed to get done without distraction. As soon as the poet's real presence was back in my life, I couldn't tolerate the country man.

The reading was held in a bookstore where chairs had been set close together. I sat in the back row. It wasn't until three quarters of the seats were taken that the poet made his appearance at the podium. I got nervous the moment I saw him. He looked a little different to me at first, somehow older, as if it had been years not months since I'd last seen him. He was wearing a tweedish-looking, out-of-date sports coat. Under the sports coat, he wore a purple collared shirt, and these two items were paired with brown pants and dark brown boots. His hair was uncombed, and his glasses were sliding down his nose. I liked looking at him, the way he was dressed, the way he stood too far from the microphone and addressed the audience with several hellos to get their attention. He said he was going to read a group of poems in succession, and we would know the beginning of a new poem because he would read the title. Then he said on second thought he couldn't be sure we'd know when he was reading a title versus another line, but he seemed unable to come up with a solution, shrugged his shoulders, and said, "Well, we'll see what happens."

I had never heard or read any of his poems before. I was relieved to find that I liked what I was hearing and that he didn't use one of those Poetry voices to recite his words. When he got to the end of the first poem he said, "That was that one. Now I'll read the next." He continued on in this fashion throughout the group of poems, announcing each one's end and the next one's beginning. After the last one he said, "That's it, thank you."

I stood at the edge of the crowd waiting for it to thin. When there was an opening, I made my way toward him. He smiled and reached out his hand for me to shake. I had never shaken hands with him before. He thanked me for coming and told me that I looked good.

"Thanks, I've been in the country," I said.

"Oh, you're rested then," he said.

"I quit the job too," I said. "I've been upstate for a few months."

"Oh, you quit too?" he said, pleased that we'd both escaped the terrible place. "A few months? What have you been doing up there?"

"Painting, sort of," I said. "I have to come back and get a job." Though the thought of returning to my apartment and going to a workplace daily felt so remote I didn't believe my own words.

I had thought I might not like him the way I had before once I saw him again, but I discovered that I liked him as much as ever. I thought of the country man, planting his garden, taking me on bike rides, serving me cheese platters, and while I had come to like him and looked forward to his company, I was always weighing whether I wanted to accept a date with him or decline and do something else. With the poet there was no weighing. I realized that with the poet I would always accept an invitation to see him without hesitation or second thoughts. And so, when he suggested that we get a drink, I accepted.

We went in and out of a couple of places unable to find somewhere that wasn't packed and loud. I said we could buy a bottle of wine and take it to his place, which we were near. He seemed to like the idea, relieved not to have to deal with the rowdy establishments, but I could see him hesitate then think better of it. "No," he said. "We'll find somewhere."

"I don't think we will," I said. "It's Thursday in the Village. Forget it."

He looked futilely at the crowds lining the sidewalks and reluctantly agreed to my suggestion. It wasn't the most welcoming invitation, but I thought once we got inside, he would relax and it would be better to be alone than out in the crowds.

Even though I'd only been to his apartment the one time, it felt like I was returning to a favorite and long-familiar place. The beat-up couch, the overstuffed bookshelves. I was happy to be amongst these things again. And the painting was still there. "You still have it," I said. "Yes," he said. "But I decided I really don't want it and I'm going to give it away. Do you want it?"

"What, now that it's free?" I said. "No thanks." He poured our wine and we sat on the couch one cushion apart.

"I'm sorry I never called you," he said. "That was wrong."

I knew we would have to talk about the night we spent together and all the time that had passed since then without a word. But I was nervous about the outcome of such a discussion. "I know," I said. "We shouldn't have let so much time go by. And you didn't have to quit the job you know."

"That wasn't really why I quit," he said. "Well, it sort of was, because I didn't feel like facing you, but I didn't feel like facing the job or my life or anything. It all kind of got tied together. Nothing was going right. I kind of hid in my apartment for a while and did nothing. Then I got sick of myself and decided to re-enter the human race as pathetic as it is. And things got better actually. I met someone. There's a girl, she runs a poetry collective in L.A., and I'm moving out there."

"You're moving to L.A.?" I said. I drank my wine and listened without understanding the poet's explanation of the collective and the part he would be playing in it. He didn't explain the situation with the girl, but I knew what it was. I wanted to say, "Stay here, don't move to L.A., come back with me to the country where we've been so happy together. You love the outdoors." But maybe he didn't. Maybe he hated the countryside and fishing and biking and preferred driving in traffic in the heat and smog. What did I know? The poet I'd spent my summer with was not the actual poet.

"I never thought I'd live in L.A., but I think I'm going to like it out there," he said.

And as soon as he said it, I could picture him there, pulling up to a taco stand in a convertible, strolling down the sidewalk in sandals, ordering alfalfa sprouts and avocados on his sandwiches. He'd live in a house with a Spanish style patio where he and his poetess would hold readings, where together they would sit under the eaves and write poems about each other. And what about me? Where would I be while all this poetry was being written and read on the sunny, tiled patio? Struggling to paint in my stuffy, noisy apartment alone, or struggling to paint in the country, at my parents' house or perhaps at the country man's house, looking out the window over his new garden and fish pond?

I finished my glass of wine, set it on the floor next to my foot and told the poet that it was time for me to go. He told me he'd send me a postcard when he got settled.

"L.A.?" I said. "It's so bright out there."

"I'll wear sunglasses," he said.

This time I opened the correct door and was able to leave without pause, though I would have preferred to make the door mistake again in order to delay my departure, if only for a moment.

Cornerstone

work by writers K-12

Saanvi Mundra

OF FLESH AND BLOOD AND DREAMS

I in the mirror—broken yet of fresher faith
the yellow of flowers and cold and juice
of crinkled sunrise with pink clouds.
the dark rivers of fate in lakes of red on palms.
from chocolate deep eyes, a rim of light
locks with my own window to soul
reflecting the dusk of memories.
old, thick toenails, dry and pale,
my chest of green rivers and
the pulp of orange, sprouting as fruit.
of smooth curves and sharper cuts
blood pumping life in a sculpture of soil
dark paths of dust to sweeter limes.
dead, waves of caressing curtains.
white husky feet, old Egyptian heels,
sweet lotus-pink lips and a sunlit smile
of scars and chikoo mango joy.
I take myself
back
from a mirror.
of flesh and blood
dreams in eyes
I rise

Kay Lee

Turtles with Teeth

there is a turtle in my back
yard.

it swims in circles with tiny webbed
feet and sometimes it will stare at
me through the tinted glass of
my window and snap
its toothless mouth against the pane.

it's cute, in an odd way, for it has
no claws or teeth with which it could harm,
swimming in circles within silver midnight wind
without-thought-without-thought-without
anything at all but the
dark.

and its beady little eyes as it stares
from the moon-
light dripping silver are wise beyond
stars-or-perhaps
that is just me and my foolish-
mind creating stories from ash
again.

my mama tells me that i am a
worthless child in
a voice that is kind-joking-screaming-rage
          and i tell her *okay* with a toothless mouth and
waterlogged lips even
as my foolish-shadowed-
mind tells her *no-no-no i am a turtle*
                    i am a turtle
                    i am a turtle-

and at night the turtle comes to my window again-
again-again-
pads its tiny feet against the
pane-snaps
harmless jaws at me in the wrenching
dark
and i
dig my nails in my skin 'till it bl-
            eeds-tear through flesh and bone with
                flattened teeth-tell myself
        worthlesschild-worthless-worthlesschild-

.

the turtle stares at me with
moonlight eyes.

i cannot help but think

mama,
                i am not
        a turtle.

Kay Lee

ROLLY POLLIES LIVE TWO YEARS

there was a rolly polly that lived
  on the side of the gray sidewalk i
    walked every morning as the sun rose
          and i did not give it
    a name, but its weight in my fingers
      was light and
              stark, as it wriggled on my skin.

                  it would curl inwards, hard
        shell pointed outwards towards
        the world, never showing
            its soft belly
                to the sun.

      and i would watch the sun rise,
every morning with
                a tiny life in my hands-
and i remember the shape of it;
 so warm a yellow, and soft, around its
    smooth edges, a
      small circle in the sky,
like a little rolly polly, curled and
afraid.

a new beginning, people
          would tell me, eyes glowing gold
  in the sun and hands warm
          in my hair, but
              the touch of the sun in the sky was never
a beginning; not for
that rolly polly and not
                for me.

it was simply a continuing;

of what- there can be no words to describe-
        perhaps some would call it *life*, or others
    hope, but
                            the sun will always rise,
and some part of me will stand,
        with that little rolly polly on the
small-town Californian sidewalk,

                            watching it waltz
    with time across the sky, and watching
        people
always step out onto the sidewalk
to face it.

Kay Lee

CUCKOO WASPS

layer your skin atop mine
one thin layer after another peeled
from spiraling skeleton
my eyes are wide and your eyes are
black and we stare at each other from across
a chasm; there
is so little in your eyes, my dear,
so little reflected back at me in a
glossy sheen.

silence has a sentience-
a twisting thing that wraps around
your shoulders and embodies
the hollowness of your flesh,
and it stares at me, through your eyes,
through the chasm, through the cool air
to the left of my lips.

(silence has a name, and it tells me this,
through your eyes, and your lips-
a sideways presence that pushes down
flat against the bed, looks down,
chases tears down the highway of my cheeks
until i crave the way you look
at me)

your flesh is made of stars,
and they gleam back at me like a terrible
imitation of something that had
been, once,
thousands of microprisms-thousands
of corroded stories refracted back from
your exoskeleton in the form
of diluted light.
and,

your footsteps *clack-clack-clack*
on the stairs, and i am hungry,
and you are at the foot of my bed,
and you taste
of nothing.

(the stars on your skin streak blurry
across my vision and i cannot bear to see
the way that you look back so i let
it blur until i am chasing the lights on the tender curve
of your flesh
in a frenzied desperation
and it burns
like nothing has ever burned
before.)

i stand
my eyes are wide and your eyes are
black

and i watch you walk away,
but then
i am still left with the chasm.

i stand
and i walk away,
but then
i am still left with the silence

Jiayi Shao

UPSIDE DOWN

It is funny how,
when you look at things upside down,
you can't tell whether
You are the problem, or
The world is.

Haile Espin

RESTLESS

I dreamt I wrote the Bible.
I dreamt that I was air.
My body fragile,
touch me I break,
hug me I crack,
love me,
I cease to exist.

Wonders slithered in my mind.
Vines grew from the cracks in my soul.
I built humans
from the tears that fell from my eyes.
I laughed
with my imaginary creations.

I chased my own soul around.
Followed it till the end of the world.
It looked back at me for a fleeting second, as it stepped over the edge.

Ants crawled out my throat.
Different versions of me screamed to be let out.
I was floating in empty air.
Gravity ceased to exist.
Chaos greeted me like an old friend.
I blinked hazily,
wondering if I should wave back.

I breathed knowledge, inhaled kindness, imitated bravery,
and stole power.
And soon, my beauty faded.
My body decayed.
And my skeleton stood there.
Not knowing who it was, who it used to be.
But it remained standing.

Henry Phoel

GOD VS GODDESS

Surrounded by pine trees on the coast of the Mediterranean Sea.
The God Poseidon stands just inches away from me.
No escape to my left but my weapon in my right hand.
To understand where this story ends, I must first tell you
    of where it began.

My reasons you will find are not hard to comprehend.
It begins with a competition, not too far from here.
The people had to choose whom they held dear.
The city called Attica is where in history we need to be.
To see the people choose She over He.

A fight over land between God and Goddess.
God of the sea and storms vs Goddess of war and wisdom.
From one salt spring to another olive tree.
It was obvious to the people who should be the chief deity.

Poseidon the God, Athena the Goddess, the people chose her.
She became their protector, their warrior, and shield
for war and wisdom were her weapons to wield.
So Attica became Athens to honor her name.
Poseidon became bitter and filled with rage.

Where do I fit in? What does this have to do with me?
In order to understand you need to know about Purity.
Athena was a Goddess but different from the rest.
The next thing you know the blade was in his chest.
He should know better than to mess with a goddess made by the best.

With anger in his eyes he stormed back to the sea.
Furious that again he had been beat.

Bravery Grace Boes

LIFE

it seems like the pine, the evergreen, is life.
seedlings grow, life.
ice turns into a puddle that helps the plants grow, life.
candlelight, that little fire, life.
a bright idea, life.

Alexander Miller

DINOSAUR

Lots of Dinosaurs with small brains,
are locked in chains.
All of the Dinosaurs, especially the omnivores
are bored.
One of the omnivores
caught their tail
in the door.
I bet
it is sore.

Matteo Tremaine Pavlenko

THE BODY

My family is like pieces
Of a body in this pandemic
Our muscles grow

And our bones get stronger
In the end we will
Be powerful together

Emma Catherine Hoff

To You I Grant My Body

1
My arms,
limbs connected to my body
by strips of bone and skin,
I shake my body vigorously,
my hair flies
in all directions,
my throat pulsates,
my wrist spasms,
my arms,
slowly they disconnect
and leave me.

2
Legs
oh, many walks I have taken
with my legs,
an extra thumb,
lengthening my body
taking from it
shape and size,
we were all born with legs,
but they were small ones,
useless,
useless forever,
take them,
for I thrust them into
the arms of the tree,
if the tree has arms
and it absorbs them,
becoming peculiar color
but taller,
reaching to the sky,

never looking back
towards the ground.

3
Little bony fingers,
fragile knuckles,
I need not be a breakable
vase anymore,
I light a match,
deep inside the folds of my skin,
underneath my little
broken nails,
and my fingers shoot
off towards
space
to orbit Saturn
and join its rings.

4
Eyes,
constantly blinking,
I give them to the blind coward
who hides,
curled up in a ball
like a hedgehog,
from society,
whimpering
and cowering,
begging
to see,
to open his enclosure,
his castle,
his barrier.

5
Lips,
oh, precious lips,
if you happened to be

ripped off,
my teeth and gums
would be exposed,
my face would be pearly
white but
bloody,
the woman with the dentures
wants lips
to contain her clacking,
her lipless face
is asking for a prize,
a treasure,
something to wear on a special
occasion,
I grant this gift.

6
Torso,
rolling around
by itself on the ground,
for the biggest foot
to kick it like a soccer
ball and run.
This haunted piece
of body
cannot be destroyed.
So hard,
so big,
it breaks every little bone
in the foot.
Gift your foot back
to me,
for that is the thing I am missing.

Notes on Contributors

Marguerite Alley (she/they) is a writer from Durham, North Carolina whose work has appeared or is forthcoming in *New Ohio Review, Chautauqua Literary Journal, Pigeon Pages, Bodega,* and elsewhere. They are an undergraduate at NYU.

Roy Bentley is the author of *Walking with Eve in the Loved City,* chosen by Billy Collins as finalist for the Miller Williams poetry prize; *Starlight Taxi,* winner of the Blue Lynx Poetry Prize; *The Trouble with a Short Horse in Montana,* chosen by John Gallaher as winner of the White Pine Poetry Prize; as well as *My Mother's Red Ford: New & Selected Poems 1986 – 2020* published by Lost Horse Press. Poems have appeared in *The Southern Review, Rattle, The Louisville Review, Shenandoah, New Ohio Review,* and *Prairie Schooner* among others. His latest is *Beautiful Plenty* (Main Street Rag, 2021).

Rebecca Bernard's work has appeared or is forthcoming in *Shenandoah, Southwest Review, Colorado Review,* and *North American Review* among other places. Her debut collection of stories won the 2021 Non/Fiction Prize held by *The Journal* and is forthcoming from OSU's press in fall 2022. She is an Assistant Professor of Creative Writing at Angelo State University and serves as a Fiction Editor for *The Boiler.*

Adrian Blevins is the author of the forthcoming *Status Pending* (Four Way Books, 2023), *Appalachians Run Amok, Live from the Homesick Jamboree, The Brass Girl Brouhaha,* and a co-edited collection of essays by new and emerging Appalachian writers. She is the recipient of many awards and honors including the Wilder Prize from Two Sylvias Press, a Kate Tufts Discovery Award, and a Rona Jaffe Writer's Foundation Award, among others. She is a professor of English and Creative Writing at Colby College in Waterville, Maine.

Don Bogen is the author of five books of poetry, most recently *Immediate Song* (Milkweed Editions, 2019). An emeritus professor at the University of Cincinnati, he maintains a website at www.donbogen.com.

Clay Cantrell holds an MFA in poetry from the University of Memphis. His poems have appeared or are forthcoming in *Sycamore Review, New Delta Review, Crazyhorse, The Journal,* and elsewhere.

Kyle D. Craig lives in Indianapolis with his wife, daughter, and an orange cat named Jasper. He holds an MFA from Butler University. His poems have appeared in *Barnstorm Journal, Blue Earth Review, The Louisville Review, North Dakota Quarterly, Sou'wester, Tar River Poetry,* and others.

Jane Ogburn Dorfman is former librarian and a storyteller living in Maryland. She grew up in New Orleans. She has two storytelling CDs; both won the Storytelling World

Resource Award. She tells mainly folk and fairy tales with a few personal stories and have lately begun telling as Calamity Jane. She's been published in *Highlights for Children* and had reviews printed in the Washington Post. A novel is being considered by Peachtree Press.

Patricia Dutt is a landscape estimator living in Ithaca, NY. She has published about a dozen short stories and recently a non-fiction book about an Iranian immigrant.

Diamond Forde's debut collection, *Mother Body*, is the winner of the 2019 Saturnalia Poetry Prize. Forde has received numerous awards and prizes, including a Pink Poetry Prize, a Furious Flower Poetry Prize, and a finalist for the 2022 Kate Tufts Discovery Award, Claremont Graduate University. A *Callaloo* and *Tin House* fellow, Forde's work has appeared in *Boston Review, Honey Literary, Obsidian, Massachusetts Review*, and more. She serves as the contributing editor of *Southeast Review*, the fiction editor of *Nat. Brut*, and she lives in Asheville with her partner and their dog, Oatmeal.

S. A. Griffin's stories have been published in *Eureka Literary Magazine, Juked, The Fiddlehead, The Journal, Cottonwood*, and *Sassy*. Griffin earned an MFA from the New School. She is at work on a novel.

Alamgir Hashmi is a widely published author of poetry and literary criticism. He has taught at various universities. For a time during the 1970s, he lived and worked in Louisville.

James Hejna completed an MFA in creative writing at UC Irvine, and then transitioned into molecular biology. He is currently an emeritus professor in the Graduate School of Biostudies at Kyoto University. Two of his poems appeared in *The Louisville Review* in the previous century.

Christopher Howell has published twelve collections of poetry, the most recent five titles from Milkweed Editions and the University of Washington Press. His work may be found in a long list of journals, including the *Gettysburg Review, The Southern Review, FIELD, Harper's, The Iowa Review*, and *Prairie Schooner*. His work may also be found in three volumes of the *Pushcart Prize*, and more than forty other anthologies.

Dennis Hurley is a retired high school English/Spanish teacher who lives and works in Michigan. He has two novels available on Amazon and Barnes and Noble: *A Sense of Place* and *The Widow*.

Edward Jackson spent most of his career as a teacher and librarian in an urban setting. Currently, he is enrolled in the MFA program at Youngstown State University. He has published short pieces in *Salmon Creek Journal, The SissyFuss, Ethel, Coffin Bell,* and *DM du Jour*. In addition, he has published essays in *The Gay & Lesbian Review, The Adirondack Review*, and *The Atlanta Journal Constitution*.

John Sims Jeter was born in Birmingham, AL and spent his working years as a mathematician and a Licensed Professional Structural Engineer. He retired in 2005 and his first published short story, "The Man Who Took Notes," appeared in the Spring & Fall 2005 issue of *The Louisville Review* 55-56 and was nominated for a Pushcart Prize. A second short story, "My Life as a Lid," was published in 2006 *Palm Prints*, a literary journal of the University of South Florida. His novel, *...and the angels sang*, was published by Livingston Press in 2007. A collection of ten short stories, *The End of a Perfect Death*, was published by The Ardent Writer Press in 2018. His works have also appeared in *Journeys of Huntsville: A Bicentennial of Alabama Statehood* and *Old Huntsville Magazine.* John served as a volunteer reader on the Radio Reading Service for the Blind at PBS stations WUSF-FM and WLRH-FM for over twenty-five years. He enjoys choral singing, classical music, and the blues. John is a member of Alabama Writers' Forum and Alabama Writers Cooperative. John and his wife, Derelene, live in Huntsville, Alabama.

Rolly Kent returned to poetry after an absence of twenty years. Previous work appeared in *American Poetry Review, The Atlantic, American Scholar, The Nation, Poetry,* and numerous other places. His books of poetry are *The Wreck in Post Office Canyon* (Maguey Press) and *Spirit, Hurry* (Confluence Press). His new book is *Phone Ringing in a Dark House.* He lives in Los Angeles.

Michael Mark's poetry has been recently published or is forthcoming in *Copper Nickel, Pleiades, Ploughshares, Poetry Northwest, The Southern Review,* and other places. He was the recipient of the Anthony Hecht Scholarship at the Sewanee Writers' Conference. michaeljmark.com

Kevin McLellan is the author of the full-length poetry collections, *Ornitheology* (2019 Massachusetts Book Awards recipient) and *Tributary.* He is also the author of the book objects, *Hemispheres* (which resides in the Poetry Center at the University of Arizona and other special collections) and *[box]* (which resides in the Blue Star Collection at Harvard University and other special collections), and the chapbook, *Round Trip.* Kevin makes videos under the name, "Duck Hunting with the Grammarian," and his video *Dick* showed in the Flickers' Rhode Island Film Festival, the Tag! Queer Film Festival, the Berlin Short Film Festival, and the Vancouver Queer Film Festival. He lives in Cambridge, Massachusetts. Website: kevmclellan.com.

Ann Pedone is a poet and literary translator in the San Francisco Bay Area. She is the author of *The Medea Notebooks* (spring, 2023 Etruscan Press), and *The Italian Professor's Wife* (Press 53), as well as the chapbooks *The Bird Happened, perhaps there is a sky we don't know: a re-imagining of sappho, Everywhere You Put Your Mouth, Sea [break]*, and *DREAM/WORK.* Her work has recently appeared in *The American Journal of Poetry, Narrative, Chicago Quarterly Review, The Louisville Review, Gigantic Sequins,* and *Conduit.*

Jack Ridl's newest book is *Saint Peter and the Goldfinch* (Wayne State U. Press) who also published his *Practicing to Walk Like a Heron,* recipient of the ForeWords Review/

IndieFab Gold Medal. The Society of Midland Authors named *Broken Symmetry* (WSU Press) year's best collection, and his *Losing Season* (CavanKerry Press) was featured on NPR. Named by the Carnegie Foundation Michigan's Professor of the Year, Jack has had more than 90 of his students nationally published several of which have won first book awards.

Mary Ann Samyn is the author of six collections of poetry, including *Air, Light, Dust, Shadow, Distance,* winner of the 2017 42 Miles Press Prize, and *My Life in Heaven,* winner of the 2012 FIELD Prize. She teaches in the MFA program at West Virginia University and lives in WV and in Michigan.

Adam Tavel is the author of five books of poetry, including two forthcoming collections: *Green Regalia* (Stephen F. Austin State University Press, 2022) and *Sum Ledger* (Measure Press, 2022). His most recent book, *Catafalque,* won the Richard Wilbur Award (University of Evansville Press, 2018). His recent poems appear, or will soon appear, in *North American Review, Ploughshares, The Georgia Review, Beloit Poetry Journal, Ninth Letter, The Massachusetts Review, Copper Nickel,* and *Western Humanities Review,* among others. You can find him online at adamtavel.com.

Gabriel Welsch is the author of a collection of short stories, *Groundscratchers,* and four collections of poems, the latest of which is *The Four Horsepersons of a Disappointing Apocalypse.* His stories, poems, book reviews and essays have appeared in hundreds of national periodicals. He lives in Pittsburgh, Pennsylvania, and works as a vice president for marketing and communications at Duquesne University.

Rachel Whalen is a poet, playwright, and translator from Buffalo, New York. They recently completed an MFA at NYU, where they were a poetry editor for the *Washington Square Review.*

NOTES ON CONTRIBUTORS TO CORNERSTONE

Bravery Grace Boes is a six year old from Northumberland, Pennsylvania. She enjoys eating avocados with salt, going to parties, and drawing. She is in kindergarten.

Haile Espin is a high school student at the Early College at Guilford. When she is not writing, she can be found in a corner somewhere, reading.

Emma Catherine Hoff is a fourth grade student at PS 24 in the Bronx. Her poems, essays, and book reviews have appeared in the *Rattle Young Poets Anthology, Stone Soup Magazine,* and the *Stone Soup Blog.* Her poetry collection, *The Immortal Jellyfish,* was a finalist for the 2021 Stone Soup Book Contest. When not reading and writing, Emma likes to hang out with her cat, Gavroche, and play board games.

Kay Lee is a tenth grader attending Korea International School in Seoul, South Korea. She is currently putting together her writing portfolio and was recently accepted into Juniper's Young Writers Program.

Alexander L. Miller—age six—a future paleontologist, might say he knows "50 bazillion" dinosaurs. When he's not learning about them, he attends St. Francis of Assisi Catholic School in Louisville, Kentucky, where he is finishing up his kindergarten year. He plays soccer for his school and is a member of the Lakeside Quarry Gators Swim Team. His other interests include reading, math, library, P. E., animals, playing on his jungle gym, and singing songs from "Encanto."

Saanvi Mundra is a fourteen-year-old poet residing in India. She is an astrophysics and cosmology enthusiast, marathoner and voracious reader who has been writing poetry for three years.

Matteo Tremaine Pavlenko is ten years old, and he loves to read books. He owns many books, and borrows library books to read too. Matteo likes to write poems, draw, write graphic stories, play soccer, and build things with Legos. Matteo is learning how to play the piano. He has younger twin siblings Bella and Luca whom he loves very much.

Henry Phoel is a 6th grader at Williamsburg Middle School in Arlington, VA. He's loved the Greek Gods ever since he did a report on the Trojan War in fifth grade. Henry also loves climbing and acting, among other things.

Jiayi Shao is a high school junior in Toronto, Canada. With a ceaseless fervor for writing, she has been writing introspective poems for several years, (will continue to do so for years to come, or so she solemnly swears) and always finds great pleasure in telling atypical stories through poetry.

About the Front Cover Artist

Joyce Garner is a self-taught painter born in Covington, Kentucky, with deeper roots in Laurel County. Garner was selected as the South Arts 2021 Kentucky State Fellow, and has had solo shows at the Thyen-Clark Cultural Center (IN); the Owensboro Museum of Fine Art (KY); the Carnegie (KY); Indiana University Southeast; the University of Evansville Melvin Peterson Gallery; the Archabbey Library Gallery at St. Meinrad; Germantown Performing Arts Centre (TN); Krempp Gallery of Jasper Arts Center (IN); the Gateway Regional Art Center (KY); Oakland City University (IN); the Headley-Whitney Museum (KY); and various galleries in Indiana, Georgia, Kentucky, Maryland, North Carolina, Ohio, Pennsylvania, and Tennessee. She earned a B.S. from the University of Kentucky.